# ALICE'S LEGACY

*GOD NEVER GIVES YOU MORE THAN YOU CAN HANDLE*

## BY KATHY GUTHRIE

Copyright © 2005 by Kathy A. Guthrie

ISBN 0-7414-2611-0

Picture on front cover by Angela Swaggard
Picture on back cover by Debra Beck
Edited by Barbara Tschantz


*Published by:*

**INFI∞ITY**
PUBLISHING.COM

*1094 New De Haven Street, Suite 100*
*West Conshohocken, PA 19428-2713*
*Info@buybooksontheweb.com*
*www.buybooksontheweb.com*
*Toll-free (877) BUY BOOK*
*Local Phone (610) 941-9999*
*Fax (610) 941-9959*

*Printed in the United States of America*

*Printed on Recycled Paper*

*Published July 2005*

In Memory of
**Alice Johanning**
**1925-1992**

**To my brothers and sisters.**
**Without you I would not have had such**
**wonderful memories to share.**

**Alice's Children**

**Nancy-March 27, 1947**

**Kathy-February 27, 1948**

**Daniel-July 23, 1949**

**David-June 22, 1951**

**Rosemary-August 19, 1952**

**Gerard-June 26, 1954**

**Marie-September 21, 1955**

**Susann-November 27, 1956**

**Gerald-March 30, 1958**

**Jane-July 12, 1959**

**Bernard-November 26, 1960**

**Vincent-September 12, 1962**

**Timothy-January 25, 1964**

**Andrew-June 23, 1965**

**Edward-April 19, 1967**

# Contents

## Acknowledgment

I extend my sincere thanks and gratitude to all the people who encouraged me to continue with this project. First of all to my sisters and brothers who allowed me to do this. To my children, Angela, Barbara, Candice, and Debra and my husband Art, who listened and encouraged me with great patience and understanding. To my friend and confidant Diane Scheuerman for her reading and her efforts to keep me on track. A special thank you to my daughter Barbara who edited the book and shared her expertise by making helpful suggestions throughout the manuscript.

Alice & Roy Johanning

# Chapter One

## *The Call*

The call comes as a shock. It really shouldn't have. Mom's had a heart attack. We should have expected it. After all, she has had diabetes for more than 20 years. We knew she had problems resulting from her illness, but it still comes as a shock when we get the phone call. Just last year, surgery to open clogged veins in her legs relieved the problems with her feet. Her circulation had become so poor she had almost no feeling in her lower legs. We should have expected that her heart would have the same problem. We just didn't want to face it.

The doctors do not expect her to make it through the night. The damage to her heart seems massive. She is now stable but in critical condition.

She's in Florida and we're in Ohio, too many miles to travel in one night. That will not stop the nine of us, more than half of Alice's children. Calls are going out, plans quickly changed, arrangements hurriedly made. We will get there as fast as humanly possible. Some will fly. Some will drive. Somehow all of us will get to Florida as fast as we can.

Frantic calling and packing, intermixed with prayers, is happening in each household. Even some grandchildren would insist on making the trip. How can this be happening to our family? After all, Mom is only 64 years old. She is active, loves to travel and is an important part of all of our lives. It's true that everyone facing a parent's illness has the same thought. Why my parent? She doesn't deserve to suffer or die young. There are so many people who love her and pray for her. Mom is the glue that holds us all together. She is the peacemaker and arbitrator of differences between

1

kids. We have always relied on her. She just can't be in pain or suffering. She doesn't deserve this.

Questions race through my mind. How is Mom doing? Are the kids in Florida with her now? How is Dad handling this? He loves her so much. They've been together so long. He needs our support.


My thoughts turn to the many talks we had with Mom about their early years together. Dad and Mom met when they were in their teens. They both enjoyed roller-skating. They met at the Land of Dance Roller Skating Rink at 12$^{th}$ St. and Market Ave. in Canton, Ohio. They loved the simple joy of gliding around the floor without a care in the world, if only for a few hours. They would do the two-step to "The Tennessee Waltz", just happy to be together. Neither of them were really good at it. They did just well enough to enjoy themselves. Mom and two of her sisters spent many nights at the rink. It was a good place to meet and enjoy others in their age group.

As Roy and Alice got to know each other, they found they had many things in common. They were both from large families, they had both quit school to go to work, and they both loved people. They enjoyed roller-skating together so much that some weeks they were at the rink almost every night.

Mom was born in North Canton, Ohio, in July 1925. She was near the middle of a family of 16 kids. Grandpa was trained as a barber but hated everything about barbering, so he made his living as a house painter. With that many children, the Depression hit them hard. Mom often told us stories of the hard times when she was young. She walked home from school on cold winter days, only to turn around, take a bucket from the porch and with her sisters, go down to the railroad tracks to pick up coal that fell from freight cars as they lumbered through town. Whenever we complained about doing without, she told us how she put cardboard in the bottom of her shoes to cover the holes and never had anything new of her own. All her clothes were hand-me-downs from her older sisters. Everything she had was shared with others. She and her sisters shared a paper route to earn money for things they needed.

But she always said she was rich in one thing, and that was family. She was close to her sisters and brothers, especially her sister Babe (Monica) and Gennie (Genevieve). They called themselves the Three Musketeers. They did everything together.

Dad was born in September of the same year. That made Mom two months older than Dad. He often teased her about being an older woman. Mom never took teasing very well, but that didn't stop Dad. He was one of the youngest in a family of nine kids. His father was a disciplinarian who expected his kids to work for their keep. Dad was not interested in school and quit after the eighth grade to work on the farm. Both Mom and Dad considered high school a luxury. Grandpa Johanning was a carpenter and taught his trade to his sons. The Depression years were not as hard on his family as they were on Mom's, but things were never easy. Both my parents grew up, as Mom would say, 'understanding the value of a dollar' and they tried to teach that lesson to us kids.

After Mom and Dad had dated about a year, Dad was drafted into the Army. It was 1944 and the country was involved in World War II. Grandpa Johanning needed Dad to help on the farm and wanted him to get a deferment so he could stay home. But Dad wouldn't agree to it. He wanted to do his duty to his country.

He was sent to California for basic training and was assigned to a Medic Unit. Being a farm boy with only an eighth grade education, he felt ill equipped for the job. He asked for a transfer and was told the only opening was in a combat unit. He gladly transferred.

It wasn't until Dad left for California that Mom realized how much she loved him. She missed him terribly and hated that he was so far away. Even keeping busy with work and the family didn't keep her from missing him every day.

They married when he was on a 30-day leave. It was a warm Ohio summer day, August 1, 1944. Mom often talked about their wedding. They were wildly happy, although Mom was mad at Dad's brothers for getting him a little drunk the night before the wedding. Growing up, I loved to look at the wedding picture stored away in the memory box. Dad looked so handsome in his army uniform. Mom, with her borrowed floor-length wedding dress swirling around her feet, was my idea of a fantasy bride. I spent many hours dreaming of wearing a dress just like hers. Mom would often reminisce about that day, surrounded by family and friends. It was nearly perfect and the war was forgotten, if only for one day.

After the wedding they went to Alexandria, Louisiana, where Dad was stationed. Mom rented a small trailer near the base and got a job as an elevator operator. Dad always says she had her "ups and downs."

Mom hated Louisiana and Dad didn't care for it either. The weather was hot and sticky and everything was damp all the time. They missed the cool fall air and rolling hills of Ohio. Both barely 20 years old, they felt too far away from the families they loved. Even being together didn't help with the loneliness and the homesickness for their loved ones.

Then a day came when Dad arrived home at the trailer with his head shaved practically bald. That was his first indication he was about to be shipped out. A few days later he didn't come back to the trailer at all. That's when Mom knew he had shipped out. The Army gave her no warning, no chance to say goodbye. He was just gone. He was sent by train to Camp Phillip Morris in New Jersey and shipped out to the European front without a proper goodbye to his bride.

Things were not going well for the Allied Forces in Europe. More ground troops were needed to push Hitler back into Germany. Dad was in a combat engineer unit on his way to the front with many other young and eager soldiers. As his ship passed the Statue of Liberty he stood at the rail wondering if he would ever see his bride again. As with tens of thousands of young couples during the war, they had to put their lives and dreams on hold.

After Dad shipped out, Mom packed up and moved back to Ohio where she could be with her family. While Dad was serving in Europe, Mom filled her time as many young wives did, producing the things needed by the armed forces. She worked several jobs during Dad's absence. But she preferred working at the Hoover Company, where she had worked before she was married. Like many young people in the early 1940's she had quit school and lied about her age to get a job when she was 15 years old. So going back to the Hoover Company during the war was comfortable for her. Her Mom and Dad and many of her sisters worked there to support the war effort. Like many manufacturers, the Hoover Company, known for its sweepers, had switched to making products for the war effort. They ran around-the-clock shifts to keep up with the demands of the growing need in both Europe and the Pacific. Every able-bodied person who wanted to work was employed. Mom told me she never knew what she was making because that was classified information. But that was OK; it was enough to know her work would help win the war and bring her new husband back to her.

Mom told me stories of gas rationing, victory gardens and doing without a lot of things to support the war. Cars and appliances made of steel were not being produced because the available metals were needed for war supplies. Most of the factories that made cars and appliances were producing guns, tanks and other necessities of war. Like most people, Mom was committed to the war effort heart and soul.

Mom's strong attachment to her family sustained her through the many months she waited for Dad's return from France. So did the many letters and pictures Dad sent home. She hurried home each day to check the mail. A letter meant he was OK, at least for now. Many letters were filled with the blacked out areas. The Army censors covered any

5

information they felt might give away his unit's location. Mom said it was frustrating to read letters that were all chopped up, but she cherished every word that got past the censors. Dad sent pictures of himself, most with the inevitable cigarette hanging from his mouth. He would be surrounded by his buddies, each holding his gun or posed on Dad's truck. Each one was a reminder of the danger he was in. Dad always loved to tell the story of how he got his driver's license. When he entered the Army, he had driven on the farm but did not have a license. His commander pointed to him and a few other guys and said "you're drivers". When Dad said he didn't have a license, the commander said, "You do now", and he was a licensed driver. As each of us kids turned 16 and took a driver's test, Dad would tell that story. Mom cherished each one of the pictures he sent home, and sent pictures of herself to him. They kept all of them in the memory box over the years.

When Dad finally returned to the United States, he was eager to pick up where he left off. On a sunny morning in May 1946 he was standing in line at a separation center near Indianapolis, Indiana, waiting to sign his release papers. Mom had driven the eight hours to pick him up in the 1940 Ford she had purchased with her wages from the Hoover Company. Knowing he was about to be discharged and his wife was waiting in the car outside, his spirits were high. This whole ordeal was almost over and he could get on with his life and start a family. As he neared the front of the line, he counted heads in front of him. Finally, only two more in line ahead of him and it would be his turn to sign the papers and become a civilian again. Then, over the PA system, he heard his serial number called. He was to report to another room. He hesitated for a moment. He looked at the line in front of him. He was just two away from signing his discharge papers. He was tempted to ignore what he heard.

He looked up again and saw that he was only one GI away from freedom. But curious as to what was happening, trained to follow orders and more than a little irritated, he reported as instructed. There was a doctor waiting to inform him of a problem with his lungs. He couldn't be signed out until he was checked by Army doctors and pronounced healthy. They said it could be tuberculosis and they would not release him unless they could rule that out. He was instructed to report to the hospital. Upset but resigned to follow orders, he did as he was told.

He spent 30 days in the hospital in Indianapolis, subjected to a barrage of tests to determine what was wrong with his lungs. Mom had driven quite a way and was not leaving without her husband. She rented a room in a private home near the hospital to stay close to him, praying every day that he could go home. Dad was permitted to leave the hospital during the day but had to report back to the hospital each night. Finally, after exhausting all possibilities, the Army decided what they had seen on his lungs was scar tissue from the pneumonia he contracted while fighting in Europe.

Though he never talked about it with us kids, Dad had fought with his battalion, the 1253 Combat Engineer's 3<sup>rd</sup> Army in Europe. During the Battle of the Bulge in the Ardennes Forest Dad contracted double pneumonia. He spent two weeks in a MASH unit recovering. When he was released from the MASH unit he had to catch up to his fighting unit.

Besides keeping him out of the action for a couple of weeks, the illness caused him to lose points. Dad explained losing points to me. Each American GI had to earn a certain number of points to be discharged after World War II. He had to stay in Europe after many guys from his unit were sent home. He needed to earn enough points to go home. So instead of returning with his unit after the war ended he was assigned to grave restoration. He was involved in transporting bodies to be sent home to their families or in many cases to be buried in Europe. Most of his time was spent in Paris and Nice. When I see pictures of the American cemeteries with their long rows of white markers I think about my Dad helping to give a proper burial to his fallen comrades. That duty was a daily reminder of how lucky he was to be going home. He could have easily been one of the less fortunate. Dad told me he thanked God every day for allowing him to return to his young bride. Getting home was on his mind constantly.

After signing papers stating that he would not hold the Army liable for his problems with his lungs, he was finally released. He received his discharge papers on June 26, 1946, and left for Ohio with Mom. After the war, like so many other couples, all they wanted was to raise a family, have a home and live the American Dream. The Bible says to be fruitful and multiply. They succeeded.

They settled in their home area in Stark County, Ohio. They bought a house on 54$^{th}$ St. in Canton for $9,500, a lot of money in those days. Dad was making 86 cents an hour working as a carpenter, building the homes needed for the returning veterans just starting families. Housing was in short supply, so Mom and Dad rented half of their house to another couple. They split the house but shared the kitchen. Each couple had a cooking and eating time in the kitchen. Mom often talked about how money was tight, but that didn't matter; they were happy. Each payday they bought a six-pack of Pepsi Cola and shared a 7oz bottle each evening as a special treat. They sat together talking about their day and the future now that the war was behind them.

They would move around the area trying to get settled on a farm. They had to start by living in the city of Canton for the first several years. Then Dad tried sharecropping to get back to the country. When he realized that wouldn't produce enough income to raise his family, he built a new house in the country and after a year sold it to buy a farm. The farm was too small, and the necessity of holding down a full-time job during the day and farming at night and on weekends turned out to be too much. With so many young children and new ones arriving all the time, Mom could not consider working outside the home, although she talked about it often. Finally they settled in the small farm town of Louisville in 1961 where Dad was able to keep a few animals and continue his work as a carpenter and cabinetmaker.

Mom and Dad moved to Florida in August 1978. By that time they were 53 years old, had been married for 34 years and had produced 15 children. Yes; 15 children. When presented with this fact many people have the same questions.

"You mean you all have the same mother and father?"

"Are some of you adopted?"

"There are no stepsisters or stepbrothers?"

"You must be Catholic, right?"

Yes, we all have the same mother and father. And, yes, we are Catholic. My parents are extremely good Catholics. To them accepting the children God sent was the right thing to do. When questioned about how she could raise 15 children, Mom always said; "God never gives you more than you can handle." We were all born between 1947 and 1967. Just a 20-year age span from oldest to youngest. It seemed that Mom was always pregnant. She was somewhat sensitive about it. When someone made a comment about her expecting another child she would say, "When I ask you to feed or clothe any of them, you can complain. Until then, don't worry about it."

Being from large families themselves, having so many children was natural to them. There were 16 children in my mother's family and nine in my father's family. Large families were just a way of life. People say large families are close. From my experience they're right. Every family has occasional differences, but when it counts my parents' families were there for each other. They helped each other with everything. There seemed to be someone in the family who could do whatever was needed; everyone shared home repairs, building projects and emergencies. When my Dad built a house, many of his and Mom's brothers and sisters were there to help. My brothers and sisters are the same way. We grew up knowing that family comes first. We can call on each other day or night to get us through rough times.

I'm the oldest. It didn't start out that way. I had an older sister, Nancy. Nancy passed away when she was seven years old from a congenital heart condition. A nun once told me an old saying, "If God takes your first-born, set a large table." She was right. I stepped up to oldest at the age of six. My sisters are Rose, Marie, Sue, and Jane.

Dan is the oldest boy. He is somewhat of a leader of the boys. There are nine of them. Besides Dan there is David, Gerard, Jerry, Bernie, Vince, Tim, Andy and Ed, the baby of the family. Nine brothers made for a very interesting life or a baseball team. Mom said with so many kids there was never a dull moment. There were many mishaps, adventures, triumphs and tribulations throughout the years. But Mom always said, "The kids keep me young."

By 1978, Dad had been diagnosed with emphysema. The cold Ohio winters were hard on his lungs, which had been damaged by his bout with pneumonia during World War II. Years of smoking and breathing in sawdust had not helped. His doctor agreed that a warmer climate would be better for his lungs, so they were Florida bound. They were never fond of Ohio weather and Florida with its sunshine and lack of snow sounded great. Some people love the colder seasons. They enjoy skiing or ice-skating and the changing of the seasons. Not my parents. They hated the ice and snow. The frozen pavement made driving difficult. They both loved the outdoors in the summer months. In Florida they would have more time to spend enjoying the sun and no frozen precipitation to fight. Dad was a skilled cabinetmaker and knew he could find work in Florida. Because they had family in Naples, they had visited that beautiful city several times. When it came to deciding where to settle, they thought Naples would be wonderful. It is so far south, the weather is warm year round and the beaches made it an easy choice. The temperature, even in the winter, is usually in the 70's compared to temperatures below freezing in Ohio. But best of all there is no snow in Naples. The West coast of Florida is less populated than the East coast and Naples is a small city tucked between the Everglades and the beautiful

10

blue Gulf of Mexico. In their opinion a more picturesque place did not exist.

Six children were still living at home, the youngest only 12 years old. The kids had mixed feelings about the move. It was exciting to imagine living in the state where they had vacationed. Yet, this meant they had to leave their older brothers and sisters. Many of the older kids were upset that Mom and Dad were leaving with part of the family. There were some hurt feelings, but we all felt that we would not want Dad to spend cold winters with lung problems. Besides, now we could travel to Florida to visit and enjoy that climate ourselves.

We held a goodbye party and cookout at Sue's house. It was a warm quiet August night, with a cloudless sky. After sundown, a multitude of stars shone as the sky darkened. Not a single leaf stirred on the trees and the cricket sang in the background. On a night like this I wondered how they could leave Ohio, and us.

As was our tradition, we all brought a covered dish. As we sat around the picnic tables in Sue's back yard, it was hard for some of us to accept that everyone would not be in Ohio together anymore. Mom kept saying the rest of us should follow them to Florida. And I believe she thought we would. There were jobs in Florida for all of us, she kept saying. We could all enjoy the freedom from Ohio winter weather. But picking up and leaving was not an option for some spouses.

I must admit some of us were a little angry that Mom and Dad were leaving. Dad wouldn't be here to advise or help the boys with projects. Mom wouldn't be here to see newborn babies or to turn to for advice and support as we struggled with raising kids. It seemed unfair.

My youngest brothers were close to my daughters. They spent many summer days together, swimming in our pool, playing on weekends and sharing great adventures. My oldest daughter Angie is a year older than Ed. My second daughter Barb is a year younger than Ed. They were as close as brothers and sisters. They sat in a group and fought tears as they talked of the fun they had together and how they would miss each other.

The party went late. No one wanted to go home. Mom and Dad and the younger kids were leaving in the morning. As long as we all stayed at the party, we didn't have to say goodbye. Finally it was obvious everyone was tired and the goodbyes would have to be said. There were tears all around. Mom and Dad promised to visit next summer, maybe for a whole month. But next summer seemed a lifetime away.

Mom insisted that we should come down to visit each year. Many of us knew that with young families to raise and not a lot of extra money it wasn't going to happen.

There was little effort to hide the tears we shed as we all hugged each other goodbye. Mom said this was ridiculous. After all, they would be back to visit. But it would not be the same. As I drove away from Sue's I had an empty feeling in my heart. I felt lost. I am a grown woman with my own family, but I felt like I was losing an important part of my life. I couldn't imagine not dropping in on Mom whenever I wanted.

When Mom was in Florida, she missed her children in Ohio. When she traveled to Ohio, she missed her children in Florida. Needless to say, they traveled between the states many times. Between visits to Ohio, Mom kept in touch by mail. My parents are from an era that believed calling long distance was a sin you are required to commit occasionally. So, calling Ohio was not an option for everyday use. Using letters, photos and children's calls to her, Mom kept in touch and involved. She was never afraid to dispense advice or express an opinion on any situation involving the lives of her children. She would drop everything and come to the aid of those needing her most.

When Gerard's baby girl died of Sudden Infant Death Syndrome, Mom headed for Ohio the next morning. Her help and support during the funeral meant so much to Gerard and his wife. Having lost a child of her own she knew they needed to rely on their family and faith in God to get through

12

their grief. When Marie was in a car accident Mom and Dad were right there to help her recuperate. They cared for her kids and helped her with the everyday things that needed to be done. When each of us started our families, she was there helping out. Now she needed us. We would be there.

Jane, the only girl in Florida, keeps us updated. The four youngest boys live in Florida. Vince, Tim, Andy and Ed all settled in and around Naples. We can imagine they are frantic. At least they are with Mom. We just cannot get there fast enough. In these situations we can do nothing but pray and support each other.

What about the kids in Florida? Are they all five at the hospital? I always think of them as children since they are so much younger. I can't help but worry about them and how they are handling the crisis. So many thoughts are going through my head as I work on autopilot to get things done. If I could just be with her and talk to the doctors myself, I might not feel so afraid.

The phone rings continuously, updating me on everyone's progress and plans. I throw some clothes into a bag, make the calls I have to make, and I'm ready to go. We just have to make it before... no, don't even think about it. If we can get there everything will be fine. We have always managed to get through everything together. Together is how we have gotten through the good times and the bad. We can get through this, together.

Plans are in full swing. Rose and Sue are first to get a flight scheduled. They will be leaving first thing in the morning. David, Jerry and Bernie will drive together. They have been very close since they were small. You always saw Jerry and Bernie wherever you saw David. Gerard will leave on a flight the next night. He was unable to make arrangements with his employer as fast as the others.

Dan, a natural leader, will drive his van and take Marie, her husband Jeff, and myself. Marie and I are happy to have the company for the trip. We decided to join Dan for moral support and economy. Three of my daughters will take a car and follow the van. With that many drivers and two vehicles we can drive straight through and get there in less than 24 hours. No one can sleep anyway. This is going to be a long and stressful ride. We leave at 11:30 p.m. From this point on, we don't know if we are already too late.

# Chapter Two

## *Nancy*

Being on the road is worse than being at home. Although we are exhausted from stress, sleep will not come. Interstate 77 South seems to stretch out forever into the darkness. The van is definitely not comfortable. For the first few hours there is plenty to talk about: Mom's condition, the trip ahead, and the problems everyone encountered in making arrangements so quickly. After a while each of us falls silent and we are left with our own thoughts. Some try again to sleep and actually succeed. For others it will be a long night. We stop a couple of times during the night to switch drivers in the two vehicles and stretch our legs. Because it is so late, we don't call anyone at our stops. We are no longer in contact with Ohio or Florida. We wonder what is going on and what we will encounter when we arrive in Florida.

In my sleeplessness my thoughts turn to Nancy. She is the one sister who will not be with us.

Nancy Marie was the first born of Roy and Alice Johanning. She was a beautiful blue-eyed blonde, barely six pounds when she was born. They were delighted with her. After the war it felt good to be happy, secure and starting a family. Mom and Dad felt blessed. Nancy was an only child for a very short time. I was born exactly eleven months to the day after Nancy. For one month of every year we were the same age. What fun it would have been as we grew up together, being the same age from February 27 to March 27; we could pretend to be twins. However, that was not to be.

Mom told me when Nancy was about six months old and she was already expecting me, they noticed that Nancy's fingernails and lips looked blue. When they took her to the doctor the news could not have been worse. Nancy had a serious birth defect. She had a hole in her heart. Enough blood did not get to her lungs to provide oxygen to her body. The lack of oxygen made her fingers, toes and lips look blue. In the late 1940s, heart repair surgery was in its infancy. Babies like Nancy did not usually live past their second birthday. The doctors gave Mom and Dad the devastating news that Nancy would most likely suffer the same fate. Without proper oxygen, the heart tries to compensate by pumping harder. Eventually it just wears out.

Mom and Dad were frantic. How could their beautiful little girl be so sick? They were determined to do all they could to help Nancy.

Nancy's birth defect made her susceptible to illness, such as pneumonia. Through her seven and a half year life she had pneumonia 11 times. But Mom and Dad were not giving up their precious daughter without a fight. When they asked the doctor what they could do to prevent her bouts with pneumonia he told them to take her South to a warmer climate. So in the fall of 1949, when she was just two years old, they rented out their home in Ohio to another couple and went to Florida with Nancy and me.

They settled in Hallandale and Dad got a construction job in Miami. Nancy had a good winter. When spring came, they returned home to Ohio. Doctors in Cleveland were making progress in repairing heart problems like Nancy's. That year, when she was three years old, she had open-heart surgery in an effort to correct the problem. She was one of the first patients in the new heart center in Cleveland. In the early '50s this type of surgery was new and still in the experimental stages. Nancy seemed to improve after the surgery and Mom and Dad were hopeful.

However, the repair didn't last. Just two years later Nancy again underwent open-heart surgery. This time they attempted to repair her heart using a vein from Dad's forearm. This was yet another new procedure to help children like Nancy. She had already outlived the early predictions of the doctors, but it was obvious it wouldn't last.

16

The new surgery was a chance to save her. Dad's vein could connect the sides of the heart properly, something the first surgery didn't accomplish.

Dad and Nancy were wheeled into the same operating room on tables side by side. Dad told me how he had looked over and saw his precious little girl, looking so small, lying on the other table. It broke his heart to see her there, so helpless. But he was willing to go to any lengths to help her. This was his chance to save her. His faith in the doctor's ability and God sustained him. He was sure after this surgery he would see his little girl, healthy and happy, grow into a wonderful young woman. They removed a vein about the size of a pencil from his left forearm and using that, they repaired her heart. My parents were relieved when the operation was a success, and they had great hopes for Nancy's future.

After the surgery her heart seemed stronger. But within two years she was again suffering from respiratory problems and even had appendicitis and emergency surgery to remove her appendix.

They had continued to go south for the winters. They locked up the house and took the growing family south in the fall and returned north in the spring. The last year they went south, they considered staying. But Mom was pregnant with their sixth child, Gerard, and wanted to have the baby in Ohio to be near her family. She was always homesick for her family when she was away from them. Dad told his employer in Florida that he was going back to Ohio one last time. They would sell their house in Ohio, settle everything and come back to Florida in the fall, this time to stay. The nomad life of traveling back and forth would be too much with six kids. If Nancy needed the warm climate, they would come back before winter and stay. So home to Ohio they went once again. In June, Gerard was born and they stayed the summer. But as fall approached, even before the weather turned cooler, Nancy was getting worse. She was too sick to travel. In September 1954, with severe pneumonia Nancy was taken to the hospital in Cleveland. She was extremely weak and her heart was failing.

In October, the doctors said without further surgery she would die. But there was hope. Her doctor had developed a plastic valve that might work. It was a new idea, but it was Nancy's only chance. On October 25, she had her third open-heart surgery.

As the doctors performed the surgery, Mom and Dad waited together, holding hands and talking softly to comfort each other. The doctors put the new plastic valve in place and everything looked good. Suddenly, while she was still in the operating room, Nancy's heart failed. The surgeon hurriedly reopened her chest and frantically massaged her heart, to no avail. She was gone. Mom and Dad knew this was a risky surgery for Nancy and they had prayed that God would spare their little girl. But all hope was gone when the doctor gave them the bad news. Now they would have to go home without her. They would have to tell us she was not coming back.

They immediately called home to share their grief with Mom's sister Babe and her husband Roy. Again, God and family would sustain them.

Nancy never realized she was so sick. Her illness was just the way things were. At the age of 7 she didn't seem to realize she would die. Neither did I. I did not expect to here that news when my parents came home.

I remember the day Nancy died as if it were yesterday. I was 6 years old. My parents were at the Babies and Children's Hospital in Cleveland with Nancy. I didn't know she was having surgery. I would not have understood if I had known about it. My parents never told me the gravity of the situation. I just thought they were with her at the hospital and she was getting better. She had been in the hospital so often it was neither unexpected nor a concern to me. She always came home when she was better. I expected her home any day and was looking forward to playing with her again.

Aunt Babe and Uncle Roy, a favorite aunt and uncle, were at our house taking care of us while Mom and Dad were in Cleveland. Their children, also favorite cousins, were there and we played and had a good time. We always did when we were with them. It was evening by the time Mom and Dad came home from the hospital. I remember it was dark outside. They brought Dan and me into the living room, and everyone else went into another room. Dad and Mom were crying. I had never seen Dad cry before and it scared me. They told us Nancy had died. She went to heaven. We wanted to know why. Why couldn't she come home? Mom said that Nancy was such a good little girl that God wanted her with him. She was up in heaven with God, she was happy and would never come back. I decided at that minute that I would never be that good. I wanted to stay here with my family. But, how could Nancy be happy up in heaven without us?

Dan was only five years old. He knew that Nancy would never come back but the concept of death was not something he understood. We cried together but his tears were brought on by fear of something he did not understand more than grief over Nancy. We went to our bedroom and cried together.

I knew Nancy was different. She was frail and her lips and fingernails were always blue. We were not allowed to play rough with Nancy. As Nancy got weaker, I could play with her on her bed or in the living room, but the boys were too rough to play with her. Nancy was my best friend. We did all kinds of things together. I remember playing on the sandy beach in Florida with Nancy and Dan before she got really weak. Walking through the surf together. Holding hands tightly so we would not be separated. I remember walking to Nancy's school in Florida, Mom pushing a baby carriage, to wait for Nancy when school let out. We walked home in the warm sunshine and Nancy would tell Mom about her day. I couldn't wait until I could go to school with Nancy. I missed her so much during the day.

But school was too hard on her and she only attended for a short time. Mom hired a tutor to teach her at home, and we didn't have our afternoon walks anymore. By the time I went to school, we lived in Ohio. Nancy was not well and the tutor came to the house there, too. I never got to go to school with Nancy, but when I got home from school I was allowed to go to our room and play with her. I would show her what I did at school and she would show me her books and papers left by her tutor.

Nancy and I always got new dolls for Christmas. We would play Mommies for hours. We would sit cross-legged on the bed and have tea parties with little metal cups and saucers from the dish sets we got for Christmas. We used water for tea and crackers for cookies. We copied what we saw Mom and her sisters do when they visited; holding our dolls, pretending to have homes and husbands.

We played outside the trailer in Florida, riding tricycles on the sandy soil around the trailer park, or watching Dad open coconuts and sharing the sweet coconut milk. It was exciting when Santa came to the trailer park, throwing candy and fruit from the back of a truck for all the kids to catch. The children in the park were so happy to see Santa. We ran behind the truck together. We never knew he was coming and the surprise of seeing him on the back of that truck was thrilling. Nancy and I hurried to the trailer to show Mom the wonderful treats we caught. We took fishing trips to the canals with Mom and Dad. Nancy and I sat on the banks of the canal and watched Dad as he threw his line in the water. On one outing Nancy lost her footing and tumbled down the canal bank toward the water. I was so relieved when Dad caught her before she hit the water. I was sure an alligator would get her. We had been warned to stay away from water where alligators might be. I remember walking on the rough grass and warm sand in our bare feet.

I sat with Nancy in the sand at the beach, watching Dad fly kites over the deep blue sea. Holding Nancy's hand in the surf so we wouldn't get swept away from each other. Mom had a rule about the water. We were never to walk into the water past our waist. Our belly buttons were the measure. Never go in deeper than that. Any further was not safe. We followed that rule on every trip to the beach. I still love the beach and spend as much time there on vacations as I can.

Both of us were too young to realize that this togetherness was not forever. We had no idea it would end so soon. Nancy being sick was, to us, the natural thing. Her trips to the hospital were a part of our lives. She always came home again.

I cried for a long time when I realized she was really gone. How could she not come back? She was my sister. She belonged with us. The idea of never seeing her again just couldn't be real. She had been there all of my short life. This could not be happening. My parents were crying. I had never seen Dad cry before and it scared me. At the age of 6 I learned what true loss was.

My cousins didn't understand. They were younger than me, like Dan. They knew something was wrong but really did not understand what death was. I just wanted them to go away. For a 6-year-old it was the end of the world.

My next memory is the calling hours at the funeral home. So many people were there. Someone other than my parents must have taken me because Mom and Dad were already there when I arrived. It seemed dark and flowers were everywhere. Mom took my hand and led me to the casket. I stepped up onto the kneeler in front of her casket so I could see inside. Nancy looked like she was just sleeping. She had on a beautiful white dress, her First Communion dress, though she never got to receive her First Communion. She was holding her white prayer book and rosary. I was sure she was going to get up and talk to me. But she didn't. I just looked at her for a long time. As I walked away from her casket people seemed to be watching me and crying. I remember thinking 'why is this happening'?

I went to a little alcove away from the crowd with Dan and we cried together. I don't know how much he understood but I knew she would never be back. It just

21

couldn't be true. I went back to the casket several times. I guess I thought something would change each time I went back. But it never did. I don't remember what my parents were doing. Only Nancy in the casket, Dan with me, and my cousins still not understanding. I cried myself to sleep in the alcove. As an adult I have attended many funerals in that same funeral home. I always see Nancy there.

I don't remember the funeral Mass at the church. But I do remember after the funeral we went to the cemetery. I watched them lower her casket into the ground. I was afraid I would forget where she was and never be able to find her again. There was a mausoleum near her grave. I took Dan's hand and we walked to the closest corner of the building and walked it off, counting each step. We had to start over a couple of times. We wanted to remember just how many steps there were from the mausoleum corner to her grave so we could find her again. I was so afraid I would forget. We never thought that we would grow up and our steps would not be the same distance. I've since forgotten how many steps it was. But I never forgot where she is. Mom and Dad had five other children at that time and medical bills to pay. A stone to mark the grave had to wait. That grave has never been marked, but Dan and I have always been able to go right to the spot. Even without stepping it off.

I have missed Nancy throughout my life. As a child I longed for her companionship. As a teenager I often dreamed of the fun we could have had together. An older sister to confide in and guide me would have been such a blessing. As an adult and mother of four beautiful girls, I often thought more of my Mother's loss and how devastating it must have been for her to lose a child. Having lost Nancy when I was so young helped me to appreciate my other sisters and my own daughters as the precious gifts they are.

So here I am. In a van, heading south, fighting back tears over my own thoughts. I need to pull it together. As the eastern sky is brightening I look over at Marie. She was the next child born after Nancy passed away. As a little girl she looked exactly like Nancy and was named Marie, Nancy's middle name. Mom always says that when Marie was born, God gave Nancy back to her. Maybe that's why they never marked the grave. We got Nancy back. Marie never knew Nancy. It's sometimes hard for me to realize that most of the other kids never knew her. They don't really think of her as a sister, as Dan and I do.

We can stop for breakfast now, freshen up and stretch our legs. I can wash my face and hopefully no one will know I've been crying half the night. At least after breakfast we will have the daylight and a little scenery to help the time pass. It looks like breakfast will be in North Carolina. Only four states to go, but they are the longest states. We still have a good 14 hours ahead of us. And we don't know what awaits us when we get there.

# Chapter Three

## *Florida*

It feels good to stop and stretch out a little. There's a long way to go. At least in the daylight we can watch the scenery. I'm taking a turn in the front seat with Dan. He's doing most of the driving.

"Dan, how's it going?" I ask him.

"OK," comes the answer.

"I don't think so. I can see how nervous you are by the way you keep drumming your thumbs on the steering wheel."

That at least got a smile from Dan, "Yeah, I'm worried and it seems like we'll never get there."

"I wonder how Mom really is right now. She's been through so much in her life. Having and raising 15 kids was no easy task. She always had something to worry about. I hate to think she may be suffering now."

"Yeah," Dan replied. "I was one of the ones that worried her the most."

"You're right there," came the comment from Marie in the back seat. "Mom was always worrying about some stunt you pulled."

Dan seemed to always be in some kind of trouble. He usually came out of it unscathed, although there were a few times when Mom wondered if she would lose him or her mind first. Dan is special to Mom. She once told me that there is always a special place in your heart for your firstborn son. Mom dotes on Dan. He was the kind of kid that could charm his way out of whatever trouble he got into. That impish grin and little sprig of hair standing straight up at his forehead would melt Mom's heart. He could explain why his antics were perfectly innocent. In contrast, he could not get away with anything with Dad. But that never stopped him from his wild capers.

"You know you were always in some kind of trouble. You even got me involved in some of your capers as kids," I said.

"Like what?' asked Marie.

I just had to tell her the squirt gun story.

Dan never took anything on faith. If a statement was made, Dan was likely to test its validity. For example, one day when we were small Dad bought us all shiny new plastic squirt guns. It wasn't Christmas or anyone's birthday, so getting a new toy in the middle of summer was a real surprise. There was one for each of us, Nancy, Dan, David and me. We heard Dad tell the neighbor the plastic was advertised as unbreakable. We had a ball, chasing each other around the yard and getting wet on a hot summer day. Dan with his impish grin and cowlick standing straight up above his forehead was running around getting the better of all of us. Nancy and I were too timid to really attack anyone and David was such a little guy he couldn't even aim straight. After a while Dan got bored with his easy prey and decided to see what would happen if we put the unbreakable squirt guns in a paper bag and smashed it against a tree. After all, they were unbreakable he said, so what could happen? It would be fun to test them. Incredibly, he talked us into it. We all gave him our brand new squirt guns and he beat them against a tree until Dad came out the front door to see what was going on. Fully expecting the squirt guns to withstand the test, Dan ran up the porch steps and eagerly handed the bag to Dad. I can still see little bits of colorful plastic fall from the bag as Dad turned it upside down over the porch floor. Shiny wet pieces lay glistening in the sun. Dan stood there in shock; from the look on his face I knew he hadn't expected total destruction.

For punishment we had to sit on the couch, not moving a muscle for what seemed like hours, while Dad sat there watching us. To take time to sit there with us meant

Dad was really mad. He was always busy with work or taking care of the yard; he never sat around the house. To have him just sit there was scary. I thought this apparently was a serious matter and things may never be the same again. It was rare for me to get into trouble and I sat there wishing I would just disappear.

I was devastated because I never got into trouble and neither did Nancy. Dan, on the other hand, took it in stride. I sat there on the couch looking at Dad as he watched us. As I went from devastated to just bored I was amazed that Dad could look back and forth at each of us and never turned his head. Just his eyes moved. Boy was he mad.

"I'm surprised you didn't get spanked," said Marie.

"Well, Dad never spanked Nancy because of her heart and I guess he didn't feel it was fair to spank the rest of us," I replied.

"Yeah, but I probably should have been spanked," laughed Dan.

Dan could talk anyone into anything. For some reason all the kids trusted him. He was the big, smart older brother. A natural leader. The others all looked up to him. You would think after the first or second time they got into trouble they would learn a lesson. David was exceptionally vulnerable. David was the closest boy in age to Dan, almost two years younger. He followed Dan everywhere when they were little. They were two little guys with unruly heads of blond hair, dirty faces, always in trouble, hanging around together.

"Remember bouncing, Dan?" I asked.

"Yeah, I remember," replied Dan. "I'll never live that down."

"Why?" asked Marie. "We all bounced."

"Yeah, but Dan started 'bouncing' in the family," I said.

Bouncing was a family tradition and a novelty to our friends. The kids sat on a stuffed chair or sofa and threw themselves back into the cushion, bouncing forward. They would sit and do this for hours, especially when they were tired. It was like rocking without the benefit of a rocking chair. Our favorite cousins, the Dimmerling kids, did the same thing. But Dan started it. I tried to 'bounce' once, but it just gave me a headache. I never got the hang of it. All the kids from Dan down to Ed bounced. They bounced in the house and in the car. Our car would rock back and forth whenever Dad stopped at a red light, as the boys in the back bounced in unison. Dad would yell from the front seat and they would all stop until the car moved again and they started all over again.

Dan took great delight in teaching his younger brothers the ropes. He taught them to catch lightning bugs, take the lights off the bugs and attach them to their fingernails. I couldn't bring myself to actually touch a lightning bug. I ran around the yard pretending to catch them. What a chicken I was! Dan made a great game of catching the lightning bugs. To this day on warm summer nights I can visualize all the little kids running through the yard on Spring Avenue catching lightning bugs.

"Remember when you broke both arms?" I asked Dan.

"Yeah, that was incredible. You know I hated it when you fed me."

"Well, it was no picnic for me either. I never got to eat."

From the back seat Marie said, "I was pretty small when that happened. Why were you feeding Dan?"

We lived on Father's Farm at the time. We lived there for about a year. Dad sharecropped the farm and remodeled the huge farmhouse when he wasn't working the fields. We called it 'Father's Farm' because our parish priest, Father Kriskow, owned it. He was the pastor at the Church we attended, Sacred Heart of Jesus in Canton. One late summer day Dan went out to the orchard to climb trees, a favorite activity of all my brothers. Dan loved being up in trees. He and David were always racing to the tops. But that day Dan was playing alone. He climbed up an old apple tree in the abandoned orchard near the house. From where Dan stood under the tree, it looked like the best apples were at the very top. Dan didn't realize, being only seven, some of the branches were dead and dead branches won't hold much weight. Dan started up, heading for the top, making good progress, when he put all his weight on a dead branch. He heard a loud snap, and the next thing he knew he was tumbling through the tree. He went straight down and landed with both arms extended out in front of him, hoping to break his fall. That did break the fall, and both arms, too.

"The pain was awful. I was crying as I walked slowly toward the house," said Dan.

I was in the kitchen, drying lunch dishes as Mom washed them, when she saw Dan coming across the yard. She looked up from the sink said 'O My God,' the closest she ever came to swearing, and ran out the door. Looking out the door, I saw Dan walking toward the house. He was crying and holding his arms out from his side. But they didn't look like arms. They went the wrong direction. You could see shiny bone sticking out of one arm and there was blood on his shirt. Mom grabbed him up carefully and sat him in the front seat of the station wagon. She ran in the house for her purse and told us to stay put. Father Kriskow was working down by the barn. Mom yelled to him to come and watch the other kids while she rushed Dan to the hospital. I don't think she even waited for Father Kriskow to answer. They were down the lane before Dan knew what was happening.

"We were saying Hail Mary's all the way to the hospital." said Dan. "Or at least Mom was. When we got to the railroad tracks at Dueber Avenue, the pain was excruciating. As I cried out in pain, Mom said her 'Hail Mary's' even faster."

They finally arrived at Mercy Hospital in downtown Canton. Dan was grateful for the ether that put him to sleep so he couldn't feel the pain. When he woke up there were plaster casts on both arms. They put a sling on each arm to hold them in front of his chest. He was now helpless. A seven-year-old, extremely active boy, totally helpless. He

couldn't do anything that required moving his arms. '
he was, both arms bent at the elbows, immobilized. E\
he could pick up something to eat, he couldn't get it 1
mouth.   He couldn't dress or undress. Worst of al
couldn't go to the bathroom by himself.

Believe it or not, the rest of us were jealous of
He was getting all Mom's attention.  Never mind that h
two broken arms; he had all the attention from Mom th
wanted.  There was never enough of Mom to go aroun(
now there was less for the rest of us.

He got extras we never dreamed of.  Soda pop \
luxury in our house.  We drank Kool Aid and seldom ;
treat of soda.   But Dan was now allowed all the sod
wanted because he could hold the nice cold bottle of
grape or orange soda securely between his two broken ;
and drink from a straw.  I think Mom gave Dan the soda
to shut him up so she could get something done.

I had the job of feeding Dan at mealtime bec
Mom had babies to feed.  I would rather have fed the ba
He hated to be fed like a baby but he was hungry enoug
stand the humiliation.  I could never feed him fast enougl
I stopped to take a bite of my own food he complained.

This happened near the end of summer.   As
beginning of the school year approached, Dan was :
panic.  Mom had to help him go to the bathroom. How c(
he go to the bathroom at school without Mom there?
thought of the nuns taking him to the bathroom
horrifying.  His friends would make fun of him.  He w(
never live it down. Thankfully, he saw the doctor before
start of school.  Mom was concerned about Dan's abilit
write and keep up with his schoolwork.  The doctor cut
cast on his right arm just below the elbow. That way,
could write.  Now Dan could bend the elbow and use
arm.   He could get dressed, write, feed himself,
thankfully go to the bathroom alone.  He would not hav(
rely on the nuns for help.

With two casts, Dan could not put his arms in
sleeves of his shirts. So Mom had to cut all the sleeves of

shirts and pin them on him with safety pins. She must have hated to ruin shirts when she had so many kids to dress. In our family clothes were cared for and passed down the line. Those ruined shirts could not be handed down to David. I'm sure she hated that. She always got all the use she could out of everything she bought.

"Marie, didn't you break an arm?' I asked.

"I did, but my story was not as dramatic as Dan's and Mom never saw me until it the broken arm was set."

When Marie was 10 years old, she had taken some of the younger boys to the playground at the elementary school. It was a favorite hangout for the kids since it was just up the road from our house. They spent hours playing on all the equipment. The area was blacktop with no cushioning if you fell. Marie was helping Vince on the monkey bars when they both tumbled to the pavement. He didn't get hurt since Marie cushioned his fall, but she landed with their combined weight on one arm. She heard it snap and felt the pain. Crying, she herded the boys ahead of her as she walked home. Across a field and past five houses, she held her arm and hurried the little boys along. Mom and Dad weren't home so the neighbors took Marie to the hospital.

"I was so scared, I just wanted Mom," said Marie.

Dan was the babysitter that day. We all took our turn as principal babysitter for those younger than us. He left the other kids with David and rode to the hospital with Marie and the neighbors. The arm was set and the kind neighbors brought Marie and Dan home. Watching Marie get her arm set and seeing her cast brought back memories for Dan. He remembered his experience with two broken arms and wanted to help Marie all he could. The Doctor told Marie to drink lots of milk for calcium to help the arm heal. Dan took this as his personal job, to see that Marie got plenty of milk. However, the doctor should have explained that she didn't need to drink all the milk right away. By the time Mom and Dad got home, Dan had coaxed her into drinking close to a gallon of milk.

Ed, the youngest, was the only other kid to break an arm, and he broke his twice. It was a sunny warm Easter Sunday. Mom's family had gathered for the holiday, as they did every year. The family holiday party was held at the American Legion hall in Greentown. Mom was having a great time, visiting with her sisters and brothers, as the kids went off to play with cousins. A cannon in front of the building attracted the little boys. They loved to climb on the barrel and sit astride it, like they were on a horse. Ed was just six years old, but he was up there with the rest of them. Someone told Ed that bees had built a hive in the open end of the cannon. He climbed to the top to get a look inside. Just as he peered into the mouth of the cannon he lost his grip on the barrel and fell, landing on his elbow. He let out a scream that brought the adults running. One of Mom's brothers got to him first and decided the arm was dislocated. As he tried to pop the elbow back into place, Ed yelled louder. In pain and terror, he just wanted Mom. With great relief, he saw her elbow her way through the crowd. Realizing the arm was broken; she carried him to the car and rushed to the hospital.

The break required surgery and two pins to hold it in place. Ed spent a week in the hospital. His birthday fell that week and he missed the regular celebration. Mom and Dad had taken him camping quite a bit and he loved it. So I got him a Fisher Price camper with little people and he played with it for hours. It was something he could handle with only one good arm. When the doctors took out the pins they let Ed keep them. To him, that was cool.

That was not Ed's first experience with a broken bone. Earlier he broke the wrist on the same arm at Springwood campgrounds. He was walking back to the trailer after an unsuccessful attempt to locate his best friend. He fell into a ditch and landed on his wrist. He knew immediately his wrist was broken. No one was around to help him so the poor little guy, crying and holding his wrist, started walking back. One of the other campers saw him and drove him to Mom. It seemed as if someone was always

31

bringing an injured child home. There were lots of other mishaps with kids. We often wondered; how did Mom do it?

I guess we all had a hand in turning her hair gray, but at the time of the many mishaps she seemed to handle things calmly. Prayer was usually her answer to any accident or problem. Whenever a car wouldn't start or she was afraid of some potential tragedy she would tell all of us to start saying our 'Hail Mary's'. She relied a lot on prayer and faith that all would be well in the end. That's what got her through so many years of raising kids.

After our reminiscing we fall silent for some time. We ride along, each with our own thoughts. The scenery is unbelievable. Weeks before we left, Hurricane Huey had hit Georgia and the Carolinas. We are amazed at the destruction along the way. We're pretty far inland and are surprised to see so many trees down. The forests we pass look like someone had taken a saw and cut the trees off at the bottoms so they have fallen in the same direction. There are damaged buildings and signs that have not been repaired.

We arrive at the border of Georgia and Florida. Our elation at being in Florida is short lived as we realize we have more than eight hours to go. We stop and call the hospital. We find that things are looking better for Mom; although she is not out of intensive care her condition is upgraded. We all say a prayer of thanks that she will be there when we arrive. We are told to go straight to Dad and Mom's house when we get to Naples. It will be late and Dad will be at home waiting for us. Sue and Rose are already there. All we can do now is keep driving and, as Mom would tell us, "say your Hail Mary's".

# Chapter Four

## *Hospital Visits*

Driving from Jacksonville to Naples means traveling almost the entire length of Florida. It is late when we arrive at Naples. Mom and Dad live in Golden Gate, an area east of Naples. Interstate 75 ends just a mile south of Dad's house. Driving through the night with windows down in the van seems foreign to us. But we are too tired to appreciate the warm temperature. Exhaustion has taken over and we are all on autopilot. Even so, it is so good to see Dad. When we pull into his drive he is up and out to greet us in the warm night air. He looks tired and drawn, but he is so happy we are there. David, Jerry and Bernie had already arrived. They got there in the afternoon and are camped out on the living room floor. One reason they traveled together is they are the smokers in the group. Dad jokingly told us that as he approached their car when it pulled into the drive, the doors flew open and a cloud of smoke bellowed from the interior of the car. He said, for a minute, he thought it was on fire but soon realized it was the accumulation from three chain smokers closed up in a car together. There are hugs and kisses from Dad and the boys, plus tears, mostly from exhaustion. Dad is emotional, and in his eyes I can see his worry and concern for his wife of so many years.

Dad fills us in on Mom's condition. Thankfully she will recover, but it will be a long time and she needs all the support we can give her. We can't see her until morning. The only thing to do is get some sleep. Dan, Marie and Jeff are going to my Aunt Jennie's house to stay. My daughters and I head for a motel less than a mile from Dad's. We need a shower and a good night's sleep. I haven't slept in 36 hours. After showering we drop into bed and sleep from sheer exhaustion.

In the morning we go straight to the hospital. So does everyone else in the family. The staff on the cardiac floor doesn't quite know how to handle the crowd. The rule in most cardiac intensive care units is two people every two hours for about 15 minutes. 'Immediate family only,' permitted to see the patient. As we all arrive, announcing we are immediate family, we start getting skeptical looks. The previous two days they had come to know the younger kids. Jane, Vince, Tim, Andy and Ed were familiar to them and they thought of them as 'the immediate family.' As we each introduce ourselves we get looks of astonishment. They finally ask in exasperation, "Is this it?" To which we reply, "No, Gerard isn't here yet."

All of the Ohio kids want to see Mom, so the Florida group lets us take the first turns. Walking into Mom's room is traumatic. The person who was always the rock, there for us, looks so tiny in the hospital bed, hooked up to wires and machines. Her face is drawn and the smile we are so used to seeing is gone. She looks so tired and much older than her 64 years, which is a shock to all of us. She is so glad to see us; I can see her eyes light up. She says she cannot believe we are all here. I don't think she realizes she came so close to dying. When she asks us why we came so far, we tell her we just want to see her and get some sun. She accepts that explanation. As each of us has a few minutes with her, the others wait in the waiting room. There are two waiting rooms on the cardiac floor, each about 10 feet by 15 feet. More like a closet than a waiting room. Needless to say, we fill the entire space in the first room. We occupy every chair sit on tables and on the floor. The boys lean against the walls and door. We insist on staying in the same waiting room. We will not consider splitting up for any reason. Every time someone else opens the door and tries to come in, there is no room. We have the room to ourselves.

Whenever her children are together Mom always brightens. Her kids, gathering around her, are good for her. But she loves to talk and she is wearing herself out with the effort of communicating with everyone. She wants us with her, but she needs her rest. Reluctantly we spend most of the day in the waiting room. Just being at the hospital helps us to feel better. Dad takes comfort in having all of us together. We spend the time catching up on everyone's lives. It has been a few years since some of the kids have seen each other. Although Mom is improving she is still in the intensive care unit and we are all concerned and worried. Even though we're enjoying each other's company, the talk in the waiting room is hushed. We are uncharacteristically quiet. Conversations are carried on in whispers.

When we picture Mom, she is sitting in one of her rocking chairs, laughing and telling stories. She loves people and being in a crowd of family and friends. It is hard to see her like this. We start reminiscing about all the time Mom spent worrying about us.

How many times had Mom been the one worrying and waiting? Of course, there was Nancy. Mom spent many days and weeks in hospitals worrying about her. There were other accidents and illness with all the kids over the years. Dan was one of the kids who caused her lots of anguish. Never on purpose, but just the same, he was a worry for her.

Like all the times he was hit by a car. Although, he says a car never hit him; he hit the cars. The first time, he was about four years old; we were living in Florida for the winter. Since our stay in Florida was temporary, we lived in a small trailer in one of the many trailer parks that populate southern Florida. He was out playing with some other kids from the neighborhood. There was a pasture across the road where cows grazed every day. The little kids were in awe of the grazing cattle. One day, the small band of adventurers decided to get a better look at the huge beasts. So they lined up, crossed the road, and climbed through the fence, one at a time. Dan was the last to cross the road. Before he took his turn climbing over the fence, someone up ahead shouted, "The cow's eating him!" That's all Dan had to hear to convince him this had not been a good idea. He turned and ran for the trailer. As he stepped onto the road, he ran right into the side of a car and bounced off the door, as the car kept moving. Almost before he hit the ground he was up and running again. Tears were already cascading down his dirty little face, more from fright than from any injury. When he arrived at the trailer and tearfully told Mom what happened she checked him over good. All he had were a few scratches and bruises. She comforted him, and then made sure he understood that he was not to cross the road. He never even played near that road again.

Not long after that we moved back to Ohio where Dan proved he really had not learned his lesson. There was a wonderful place we loved to visit in Canton, Grandma Foltz's house. Grandma Foltz had a magnificent red brick Victorian house in the city. We loved that house. There was a wooden staircase with 19 steps to the second floor. There was another smaller set up to the attic. The steps were so wide we could lie down across one without bending our knees. It had a long banister we could climb on at the top and slide all the way down to the front door. We played for hours on those stairs. The big wraparound front porch had a swing that would hold six kids. And on the back porch there was a glider and lots of chairs where the adults would sit and talk and laugh all afternoon. That's where Grandma served us homemade cookies and milk or lemonade. Because Mom came from such a large family, there were always cousins for us to play with. We would rather be at Grandma's house than anywhere else on earth.

One afternoon we were playing in Grandma's big back yard. There was an alley between Grandma's house and the house next door, which was converted to apartments. There were more kids there for us to play with. That day we were playing tag. As Dan ran across the alley to avoid being 'it', he ran right into the side of another car. Thankfully the driver was cautious since so many kids were playing near the alley; his car was barely moving. Dan again escaped serious injury.

Later that same summer we went on a Sunday picnic at Atwood Lake. It was a beautiful day and we looked forward to the picnic and a day of swimming in the lake. Parking spaces were in short supply and Dad pulled onto the grass across the road from our picnic site. Dan had learned his lesson about running across the street. However, just to be safe, Mom reminded him to be careful. He looked to his left and saw that a car was coming. He determined that he had plenty of time to cross the road. As usual he took off as fast as his little legs could go. Unfortunately, a car was coming from his right. He ran smack into the side of that car.

The driver was going so slow he was able to come to a dead stop when he heard the thump on his car. He didn't know what happened. When he stopped, his back tire was on Dan's foot. Dan was lying on the ground, with the tire pinning his foot to the road, screaming at the top of his lungs. Mom dropped what she was carrying and started yelling at the driver. "You're on his foot! You're on his foot!" With his window up, the poor driver didn't know what was going on. When he finally backed up and freed Dan, he was understandably as upset as Mom. A trip to the hospital revealed there was no real damage to Dan's foot. We think he has finally learned to look both ways before crossing the road, as he hasn't hit a car in a long time.

David had a hospital experience to share with everyone, too. He once had a mysterious illness that caused Mom many sleepless nights. David was a very active, wiry kid. He never sat still. He was a bundle of energy constantly on the move, building things or taking care of his many pets. He helped out around the farm from a very young age just like Dan. Although Dad expected more of Dan since he was the oldest he still put plenty of responsibility on David.

David loved to run. He could jump off a wagon in the field and outrun a rabbit. The poor little bunny would give up from sheer exhaustion.

One morning, when he was about six years old, he awoke unable to move any part of his body. Mom and Dad took him to the doctor, who immediately put him in the hospital. They suspected polio. In the 1950's we were warned about the virus all the time. Our cousin, Dick, had polio and Mom feared one of her kids would get it, too. What a relief for her when we were able to get vaccinated for it. In David's case it wasn't polio, but since they did not know what the problem was he was quarantined at the hospital. This meant he was all alone, something David wasn't used to. He missed his brothers and sisters terribly. He hated lying there in a hospital through the lonely nights. As kids we did not like to be separated.

Since he was sick he got a lot of toys from family and friends, things he wouldn't have otherwise received. There were coloring books and storybooks, toy trucks and cars, but that was no consolation to David in the hospital. He just wanted to be home with the family. The doctors ran every conceivable test on him. Everything they could test was ruled out as the cause. Slowly he got better and they never could tell what had caused the problem. He was finally sent home without a diagnosis. However, the toys had to be destroyed because they still had no idea what caused the problem and if it might have been contagious. With the polio scare of the 1950's my parents were not taking any chances. The loss of the toys was a disappointment to David. Not because he didn't get to keep them, but because he had looked forward to sharing these new treasures with his brothers and sisters.

When he left the hospital the doctor teased him and told him to be good and drink lots of root beer. That's all he needed to hear to pest Mom to take him to the root beer stand on the way home from the hospital. That was a great treat because Mom and Dad didn't have extra money to take kids places like that. This was an adventure he could tell the rest of us about. He got to eat lunch from a tray attached to the car window. How nifty was that? Feeling so special gave him a real lift and something fun to talk about. After he got home things got back to normal and he continued with his favorite activity, tormenting Dan.

Mom's trips to the emergency room were pretty regular as we were growing up. I often wonder how she kept her sanity. Sometimes an accident happened right in front of her and she was powerless to stop it.

Rose added a number of gray hairs to Mom's head one spring day after school. Mom was driving up Main Street to run an errand as Rose was walking home from school. Mom saw her and honked her horn to get Rose's attention. When Rose saw Mom, she said goodbye to her friend, and ran across the street without looking for traffic. A car was approaching from the other direction. It struck Rose as Mom watched helplessly from the driver's seat of her car. Rose flew over the hood of Mom's car and landed against a large tree trunk. Mom was in shock for just a few seconds. As Mom got out of the car, Rose jumped up off the ground, grabbed the tree, and shouted, "I'm not dead, I'm not dead." She was sure people would think the impact had killed her, and she wanted there to be no question, she survived. Mom ran to her and calmed her down. Although Rose protested, Mom insisted she go to the hospital to be sure she was not hurt. She managed to have only some bumps and bruises; nothing was broken from the impact. Mom said she would never flag down a child again.

Jerry had a traffic mishap to share, also. A car struck him while he was riding his bike. He was going to Dad's shop when it happened. Dad was a carpenter and cabinetmaker all his life. In 1966 he bought a cabinet shop and went into business building kitchen and bathroom cabinets for new homes or for people who wanted to update their old house. The older boys worked in the shop, helping Dad build the cabinets, and the younger ones did cleanup work. Jerry was one of the younger ones and rode his bike to the shop each afternoon to clean up. As luck would have it that afternoon, Mom happened along on her way to see Dad just after the car hit Jerry. The bike was pretty banged up and Mom was shook up, but Jerry was fine.

Jerry was an adventurous child, but usually he tempered his adventurous side with caution. He was a quiet little guy who seldom caused any trouble. However, being a typical boy, he didn't always think before acting. Camping out in our back yard or the neighbor's was a favorite pastime for all the boys. One spring night Mom allowed them to camp out at a neighbor's house. Mom cautioned them to be careful, not to leave the neighbors property and to listen to the adults. Her usual speech. Jerry picked up his camping gear and hurried next door. It was early spring and as the sun went down it got cooler. The boys wanted a fire and Mr. Goffus, the neighbor, assisted them in building the first campfire of the year. As they sat around the fire telling stories the fire slowly died down. They added wood but were not satisfied with the fire. One of the neighbor boys thought that adding a little gas to the fire would make it burn. Going to the garage, he got a can of gas and brought it over to the fire, which had begun to burn the fresh wood they had added. As the kid poured the gas directly on the flames, the fire followed the stream of gas up to the can. His first instinct was to throw it. The can landed on Jerry, and his pants caught fire.

He did the first thing that came to mind. He ran. By the time the other boys could catch him and put the fire out, his legs were badly burnt. Now they had a dilemma. They could not admit what they had done without getting into trouble. If their parents knew what had happened there would be no more campouts. The neighbor boys talked Jerry into keeping quiet about the incident. But the pain was so great he had to go home to Mom for help. She and Jerry spent the night in the emergency room. Thankfully the burns were first degree and healed quickly.

So here we are, waiting our turn to see Mom in the hospital. Spending the time telling stories about growing up, we get a little taste of what it was like for her all those years. All the times she sat with us at hospitals or tended to us when we were sick, holding our hands and telling us everything would be all right. Her faith and convictions that we would recover made us believe her. I wish we could believe it now. We know she has a long road to recovery. We will be there for her.

# Chapter Five

## *Feeding the family*

I have mixed feelings at the hospital. It is wonderful seeing all my brothers and sisters. I just wish the circumstances were better. The boys who live in Florida seem so different. To me, the oldest, they will always be little boys. I had fed, bathed, and diapered most of them. We were never all living in my parents' home at the same time. Nancy died before anyone younger than Gerard was born. I married and moved out before Ed was born. 13 was the most we had in the house at any one time. Even that is an incredible group. Meal times were always chaotic. Mom never had to call us to dinner more than one time. Everyone knew if they dallied they would lose out. She always said if anybody didn't want to eat what she served, there would just be more for the rest of us. So there was a stampede for the table whenever she announced that dinner was ready. Looking at all these healthy young men in this hospital waiting room, I can't help wondering, "How did Mom do it?"

She did an unbelievable job of feeding her brood of hungry kids. When we lived on farms we grew most of our food. We raised our own beef, chickens and hogs. Dad raised animals to sell and for the table. He did his own butchering. We all helped with the gardens and the animals. The boys had chores in the barn and the girls helped in the house. That's the way it was in our house. There were girl jobs and boy jobs. The boys wouldn't be caught dead doing 'girl work'. No one wanted to be called a 'sissy' by his brothers. Even though some of the girls wanted to do boy chores in the barn, Dad would not allow it. Girls were allowed to work in the fields at harvest time, since all hands were needed to get the crops in.

Mom canned and froze much of our food. We had three gardens. The early garden was for peas, beans, green onions and leaf lettuce. The regular garden contained pepper, tomatoes, green beans, cabbage and corn. Then a late garden had beans, potatoes, carrots, turnips, pumpkins and cabbage. We had fresh vegetables all summer long. The girls spent many days in the summer and fall helping put up vegetables and fruits in quart mason jars. Fruit was abundant on the farm. We had grapes and raspberries for jelly and jam. Mom made the best you ever tasted. My favorite was red raspberry. It was like eating raspberry right off the bush, except sweeter. Grape jelly was Mom's favorite and she made plenty of it. With her preserves, our regular school lunches of peanut butter and jelly sandwiches were a little more bearable. Mass-produced jelly and jam couldn't hold a candle to Mom's homemade with paraffin melted and poured on top of the jar to seal in the flavor. We had peach, apple and pear trees. The canned applesauce, peaches and pears lasted most of the winter, if the boys didn't steal too many for their campouts. Dad was proud of his homemade sauerkraut and ketchup. We had a bottle capper that crimped the caps on the ketchup. The caps were like the old soda pop or beer bottle caps that had to be opened with a bottle opener. We had as much fun capping the bottles as we did eating the ketchup.

We churned our own butter from the cream skimmed from fresh milk. Everyone had to help turn the crank on the big glass butter churn. After just a few minutes of vigorous churning, our arms would begin aching and soon the burning sensation would set in. Then we cranked slowly until Mom reminded us to speed up. To get butter from cream we had to keep up the pace. We also used the sweet cream to make homemade ice cream. It took a lot of kid power to turn the crank on the ice cream maker, but the end result was worth it. That sweet grainy ice cream with home made natural flavor and rich butter fat was a heavenly treat by any standards. For some reason turning the crank on the ice cream maker was not nearly as tiring as the butter churn.

And Mom baked. She loved to make bread, cakes, and cookies. And her pies were delightful. They were her specialty. She made some fillings from scratch like cherry, peach and apple. They were never too sweet, allowing a fresh and natural taste to the fruit filling. Her piecrust was never tough. As she worked at the counter making pies she would tell me, overworking the dough would make it tough instead of flaky and light. She knew just how much mixing and rolling was needed. I never learned to bake a good pie when I lived at home. She loved making them so much she wouldn't turn the job over to anyone else. I was taught to bake everything else, but pies were hers alone. On Saturday mornings she baked as many as twelve. When she finished they were lined up on the counter to cool. The aroma of fresh baked pies overrode the smell of the Murphy's Oil Soap I used to clean on Saturday mornings. She made traditional pies like apple, cherry, peach and pumpkin. But Dad loved different fruits, like raisin or pineapple. With so many mouths to feed we could consume two to three pies at one meal. It's a good thing Mom loved baking.

Her homemade noodles were a treat. Good noodles take lots of eggs and Mom never skimped. We had three large geese that laid huge eggs in the tall grass along the garden. The strong taste made them unappealing for breakfast, but they made the most rich, delicious butter yellow noodles we ever tasted.

Mom knew hard-working farmhands of any age needed food and plenty of it. The volumes of food Mom cooked required kettles, not pans. My friends would correct me if I mentioned putting a kettle of potatoes on to cook. They informed me, as did my Home Economics teacher, we cook in pots and pans, not kettles. Well maybe they did, but most of our meals were prepared in kettles much bigger than the little pots and pans we used in Home Ec. I was the chef's helper at home. I peeled potatoes, sliced bread, set the table, and did general clean up. There were piles of dishes to wash and dry. All the girls had to help.

We never went hungry. When we were growing up, we thought "store bought" food in our friends' school lunches was cool. We were amazed at how easily they traded their "store bought" lunch for the homemade goodies we didn't appreciate. We thought Scooter Pies and Twinkies were luxuries. Oreo cookies with creamy fillings were easily traded for Mom's homemade chocolate chip cookies.

Dad liked to sit at the table and point out all the food we grew ourselves. He bragged about how little of the food on the table came from a grocery store.

We all helped to provide these home grown meals. Everyone had to weed and hoe in the garden. We were assigned a row to weed, and we raced to the end. The sooner we got done, the sooner we could go play. When harvest time came we all pitched in. The best time to work in the garden was early in the morning or in the evening when it wasn't so hot. Mom enjoyed getting out in the garden. I hated it. There were bugs, it was hot and sweaty, and there was dirt. I would do anything to get out of it. I volunteered to watch the babies so Mom could go to the garden. She enjoyed the break from baby bottles and diapers and I escaped the dreaded outdoors.

We raised our own animals for meat. Because we were such a large family and didn't have extra money, many people assumed we didn't eat well. For example, a friend of Jerry's invited him to dinner and announced proudly, "We're having steak; I bet you never get steak." Jerry just shook his head. Not only did we eat steak regularly, Jerry hated steak.

Wednesday was spaghetti night. Everyone loved Mom's spaghetti. We brought friends home for meals, and spaghetti night was a favorite. More important than the food, I think our friends liked the atmosphere. Everyone talked at the same time. They could join several different conversations going on around the table at any given time. The noisy joy was infectious. It was fun just to sit back and watch everybody enjoying each other's company and the homemade breads and desserts.

Sunday dinner was special. It was always a big meal with all the trimmings. After church we spent the entire morning preparing dinner. My job was usually to peel and mash potatoes. Preparing potatoes for up to 15 people was a major undertaking. I would drag thc sack of potatoes from the storage area on the enclosed porch to the sink, dumped some in to wash and start peeling. It seemed like a never-ending task. But as long as I had a radio to listen to I was content.

We loved it when Grandma Johanning came to Sunday dinner. Grandma was amazing to us kids because she didn't have any legs. When she was a young woman her legs were amputated above the knees. Dad, or one of the boys, when they were old enough to drive, picked her up after church to spend Sunday with us. She sat in her wheelchair (which fascinated us) at the end of the table. She was always dressed up with every strand of her naturally curly hair in place. She wore makeup, which Mom almost never did, and looked so pretty. She had a fancy lace and embroidered handkerchief tucked in the sleeve of her dress. She said a lady should never be without one, as you never know when you may need it. She always smiled and agreed with anything you said. She looked like a very proper lady from a time gone by. She usually spent the whole day in the chaos of our house. By the end of the day she could often be seen using her fancy handkerchief to hold the ice-cold bottle of beer Dad offered her. She loved her single bottle of beer in the evening. She told me her doctor prescribed it to help her sleep, and it worked. We always tried to be on our best behavior when she was there. We never wanted Grandma Johanning to think we were not little angels.

Sunday supper, the evening meal, also drew guests. We would have sandwiches and maybe chips, but what was special about Sunday supper was ice cream. If we didn't make it ourselves, we bought it. Besides birthdays, Sunday was the only day we ate ice cream, a special treat. We had an abundance of healthy meals, but junk food like ice cream, candy, and chips were for special occasions. Dad was the one who welcomed people to meals. Mom was a little less enthusiastic about it. After all, the groceries had to last all week.

Not all meals were a party. If Dad was in a bad mood or had an argument with Mom, dinner could be tense and quiet. If any of us was in trouble, usually the boys, silence was in order and the meal seemed to last forever. Bad report cards, notes from a teacher, chores not completed, or one of the many incidents that solicited a 'wait till your Father gets home' response from Mom caused a tense meal. All heads would be down and the only sound you could hear was cutlery hitting china. The sooner the meal was over the better. Everyone wanted to escape to other activities. Even homework was a welcome diversion.

Before every meal Dad would say grace. We never ate a meal without saying grace. The tone of his voice as he bowed his head in prayer was our cue as to how the meal would go. A light quick tone meant he had plans for the evening and dinner would be quick. A stern tone; someone was in trouble. A slow pace and soft tone foretold a leisurely dinner with lots of conversation. That was another benefit to bringing a guest to dinner. Mom and Dad did not believe in letting company know there was anything amiss in the household. I was amazed that they could be having a disagreement, actually arguing, someone would drop by the house, and our home became a utopia of happiness. Welcoming smiles, lively conversation and maybe a few card games filled the evening. As soon as the guest left, the disagreement continued as if there had been no interruption.

Our meals were eaten as a family, together, at the kitchen table. And everyone ate the same thing. If we didn't like what was served, we could either eat it or go hungry. Dad said "a family that eats together, stays together". For every meal the table was set and the food was presented in serving bowls. After grace, the food was passed around and everyone dug in. I sometimes visited friends' homes where meals were eaten in front of the TV or everyone came to eat when they felt like it. They went to the stove and filled their plate directly from the pan. This amazed me. How could they do that? Didn't they want to talk about their day? Didn't they want to be together?

When we set the table, putting all the plates and tableware at each place, then adding the bowls and platters of food in the middle, it was overflowing. On the farm we had a chrome and Formica dinette table. It was a typical 1950s model, with shiny chrome legs and a Formica top that could withstand the punishment of kids with tableware in hand. It had two leaves that, when added made it longer. We kept the leaves in the table, so it was fully extended all the time. Dad had built a bench along the wall for five kids to sit. He sat at one end and Mom at the other. Chairs lined the other side of the table and there was always at least one high chair next to Mom. One summer evening we had the table loaded as usual, and had just sat down to steaming bowls of food waiting for us to finish with grace. Dad started saying his usual prayer. As he spoke quietly, we heard a cracking sound. Amazed, we watched, as very slowly, the middle of the table started to sink and the four chrome legs began to spread outward. Large platters and bowls of food began sliding toward the middle of the table. Mom yelled, "Everybody grab something." As we each grabbed what we could reach and stood up, the table crashed to the floor, dishes and tableware piled in a jumbled mess in the center of the fallen table. The little ones started crying as the rest of us stood there in shock, holding bowls of hot food. Mom recovered first and told us to set everything on the kitchen counter. Then we made up plates and went out to the porch to eat. Dad did a temporary fix on the table that night.

The next day he began building an indoor picnic table to replace the battle-worn chrome and Formica table. The legs of the new table were wrought iron; the benches and tabletop were wood, covered with Formica. The entire thing could be wiped clean easily. Only two chairs were required, one at each end for Mom and Dad, and six or seven kids could sit on each side.  Mom loved it.  It served as our kitchen table for years.  It was a novelty, friends and family enjoyed sitting around it as much as we did.

We each had a regular place at the table where we sat for all meals.  The girls sat on one side and the boys on the other.  As the family grew, there were soon more boys than girls and some of the boys had to sit on the girls' side of the table. I sat in the middle of the girls' side.  We were taught to always say please and thank you.  If you wanted something, such as the butter, you were to say, "Please, pass the butter".  Without the please we didn't get what we wanted. Because I sat in the middle, and was the oldest, I ended up passing everything to everyone at the table.  I often didn't get to eat since I was so busy passing things back and forth.  One day, disgusted, I decided I wasn't going to pass anything to anyone just to see if someone else would take over the job.  As kids asked for things, I ignored them.  That lasted about five minutes, then Dad said, "Kathy, can't you hear them?"  From then on I just passed things.

The kids who sat near Dad were blessed.  He was energetic when it came to using a salt or peppershaker.  Not only would his plate of food get a generous coating of salt or pepper, but also any plates near him.  I was glad to be sitting a few places away from Dad.  Mom had the two smallest kids on either side of her.  I don't know how she ever got to eat; she was so busy feeding little ones.

We ate a lot of hamburger.  It simply went further than any other meat.  We thought Mom made the best meatloaf, Swiss steaks, spaghetti, and chili in the world.  I remember Mom's chili fondly.  But some of the kids didn't like the beans in the chili. They would pick them out and add them to Dad's bowl. He didn't care; he loved beans.

We always ate at home.  Most of the kids never stepped into a restaurant until they were teenagers. Dad said going out to eat was a waste of money.  What he actually said was "It costs too much and usually isn't any good anyway."  I guess Mom's home style cooking had him spoiled.  Quite often I have found his observation to be correct. I was about 10 years old when I had my first experience in a restaurant. I had spent the weekend with my cousin, Carolyn who lived in town. After Sunday Mass, Aunt Jenny and Uncle Mick took the family to a home-style restaurant, packed with diners. They told me the food would be great; it was like Grandma used to make. I was looking forward to it, though I was nervous because I had never eaten in a restaurant. When the food arrived there were comments all around the table about how great it was. I was confused. This is how we ate every day. Besides, the place was noisy, the tables were too close together, and I felt I needed to rush through the meal so the people standing at the door could have a turn. I just didn't see what was so wonderful about eating in a restaurant.

I was the designated lunch packer in the mornings. I would line slices of bread up on the counter, spread peanut butter, then jelly, slap on the top slice and wrap the finished sandwiches in wax paper. Home baked cookies or cupcakes went next, then fruit. Whatever was available was packed in lunches that day. We had delicious pears and plums in the fall. Apples stored well through the winter, so we had them most of the time. After school I begged Mom to let me bake cookies for the next day's lunches, if Mom hadn't done them. I loved to bake.

Mom said kids slept better if they have a bedtime snack. We had one every night. We also had after school snack to hold hungry kids over until dinner. But the best snack time was afternoon snacks in the summer. We took saltshakers to the garden and picked fresh tomatoes and ate them, letting the juice run down our chins. Sometimes Mom joined us. She cut and quartered cabbages to eat right in the garden. When fruits were ripe, we climbed the trees and ate our snack sitting in the limbs. Apples were Mom's favorite. She also loved popcorn. We popped it in a big Dutch oven, which was emptied and filled again. Kool-Aid was the snack drink. Soda pop was a luxury reserved for special occasions. Mom's favorite Kool-Aid flavor was root beer and she bought it all the time. I hated it and so when I went shopping with her I tried to pick other flavors, too.

Although we grew everything we could, and Mom did a lot of baking, we still needed to buy some items from the store. And when we moved off the farm, we had to use more 'store bought' food. Mom was a champion bargain hunter. She watched the paper for specials and took advantage of all the sales she could find. If bread was on special at 10 loaves for a dollar, she drove a half dozen of us to town, gave each of us one dollar and sent us marching into the store. Each kid would buy 10 loaves of bread (the store's limit). Six kids equaled 60 loaves for six dollars. With that many kids, we needed that much bread.

Mom stored most of the bread in the big chest freezer along with all the meat and vegetables. But it wouldn't last very long; we could go through two to three loaves a meal.

Making toast for breakfast was a challenge. A two-slice toaster couldn't keep up with the demand; we would be making it all morning. Mom taught us to use the oven. We put as many slices as possible on a broiler pan and slid it under the preheated broiler. We stood there, with the oven door slightly open, to watch the bread. As soon as it browned, we quickly pulled the pan out of the oven, turned all the slices over, and slid it back under the broiler. We stood there to watch the other side because no one wanted to be responsible for burnt toast. Bread was never wasted. If the toast was burnt, we scraped off the blackened area to salvage it. We learned at a young age that 'there are starving children in China who would love to eat burnt toast'. Relax our vigilance for even a few moments, and the bread would be black. And each kid would come down to breakfast with the same question, 'Oh, man! Who burned the toast?'

Another reason bread never lasted long at the house was a trick the boys played. Every once in a while they got mad about some real or imagined injustice, and decided to run away. They always knew, when running away, the most important thing to do was provide for the next meal. They snuck into the kitchen, made peanut butter and jelly sandwiches and took a few cookies. Then they took off across the field. They seldom actually left the farm. They usually ended up in the woods, at the back of the property, where they played some war games, ate their carefully packed meal and headed back to the house by suppertime. But it was always a great adventure and got them out of Mom's hair for a while.

Bananas were a favorite fruit. Mom always waited for a sale to buy bananas. We couldn't grow them and they were a treat. When any store in town advertised 10 pounds for a dollar we were on our way. It was a little more difficult to give each of us a dollar for 10 pounds. It's hard to buy exactly 10 pounds. We piled bananas on the scale, added a big one, took off a small one and rearranged the pile of bananas until it came out to 10 pounds. Then the next kid started his pile. This did not endear us to the store manager.

Mom shopped at the same grocery store for her regular weekly shopping for many years. One of the bargains was their weekly nine-cent item. If you purchased 20 dollars in groceries, they offered a special item each week for just nine cents. If the special was something Mom could use, she divided her week's shopping into more than one cart and had kids get in a different checkout lane. We were seasoned grocery shoppers before we could see over the grocery cart handle.

Mom also taught us her philosophy concerning manufacturer's use directions. She explained the difference between how much you really need, compared to how much the manufacturer of the product said you should use. For instance, a bag of chocolate chips has the recipe for cookies on the back. Mom doubled all the ingredients in the recipe except the chocolate chips. We thought everyone did that. When measuring laundry detergent, if a cup was called for, Mom used three-fourths of a cup. According to Mom, the manufacturers wanted us to use the product as fast as possible so we would need to buy more. It was a marketing ploy, and she did not fall for wasteful marketing suggestions. I still make Kool-Aid with only three-fourths a cup of sugar instead of one cup called for on the package. Any more than that is wasteful.

I have never known anyone as good at bargain hunting and saving as Mom. Living through the Depression and a World War taught her to economize.

All this talk about food is making us hungry. Most of us haven't had much of an appetite since Mom's heart attack. Talking about food seems to bringing back our lost appetites. We won't be able to duplicate the foods we remember Mom making, but we can join Dad in the hospital cafeteria for dinner. The break from this crowded room will do us all some good.

# Chapter Six

## *Confessions*

As we join Dad in the hospital cafeteria for dinner, I am surprised to see it is fairly empty. I guess hospital cafeteria food isn't all that popular. We quietly line up and fill our trays with selections from the counters. To sit together we need to push two large tables together. After the sound of chairs scraping on vinyl flooring and the clatter of plates and cutlery being arranged, the room falls silent. We each surrender to our own thoughts while we quietly eat. I glance over at Dad, near the end of the table, and notice the dark circles under his eyes. He looks tired and much older than just a few months ago. Mom and Dad are one of those couples who may have their differences over little things, but are really close. They are never apart for long. Dad often brags that he and Mom have seldom spent a night apart since the war.

As the boys get a little nourishment and start feeling better, they become talkative again. The conversation starts out quietly, but is soon lively. Dan is telling the younger boys about some of the stunts he pulled as a kid. Many of the stories Dan is telling, Dad is hearing for the first time today. He shakes his head and smiles as the stories pour out.

Of course, Dan is the ringleader in most of the stories. I'm surprised he's telling some of this stuff. Most of it has been well kept secrets among the kids for years. I guess he figures being a grown man, with two kids of his own, he's definitely too old to spank.

"Remember that great Farmal M tractor you had back on the farm in Carrollton?" Dan asks Dad.

"Sure I do." said Dad. "That was a good piece of equipment. We worked that tractor hard."

Well, Dan had a secret to tell Dad about that great old tractor. We lived on the farm in Carrollton for 3 years. Dan was only 8 years old when we moved to the farm, but as soon as he grew tall enough to reach the pedals, Dad taught him to drive a tractor. Dan loved the power and the grown-up feeling of driving through the fields and around the barn. He could never get enough 'drive time.' Occasionally, Mom and Dad needed to be away from the farm together and they would leave me in charge of the kids. Dan could hardly wait for the dust to settle on the lane before he was out the door and up on the tractor. He proudly started it up and drove all over the farm. Dad never let Dan drive the tractor unless he was there to supervise. But when Dad was gone, Dan saw his chance to drive alone and show off for his brothers. He was in heaven on the tractor seat.

This was a nightmare for me. I wasn't concerned about Dan getting hurt or having an accident. I knew he was a good driver. I was scared to death Dad would find out and kill him. Dan seemed to have no fear of 'death by Dad,' but I was terrified. I begged him not to drive the tractor, but my pleas fell on deaf ears.

At the top of the lane, near the barn, was a big red storage tank resting on four steel legs. Gasoline was delivered to the farm and stored in the tank for the tractor and other farm machinery. Dad would pull up to the tank and fill up from the hose and nozzle hanging from one end. When he needed to fill a piece of farm equipment, gravity did the work, and no gas pump was required. When Dan needed more gas for his joyride he just filled it up. He always carefully questioned Dad to determine how much time he had to enjoy himself before they returned. When he figured Dad was due to arrive home, Dan carefully parked the tractor exactly as he had found it. He took great care to get the tractor wheels in the exact spot they were in when Dad left. Dad never realized it had been moved.

Dad did eventually notice, however, that the storage tank of gas was not lasting nearly as long as it should. He seemed to be using an awful lot of gas on the farm. So he started measuring the gallons of gas he used and compared that to the number of gallons on the delivery bill. They didn't match. It appeared that Dad was getting shorted on his deliveries. The next time the delivery truck came up the lane, Dad jumped up from the table and hurried out the door to confront the delivery driver. Stalking out to the tank, shoulders squared, with a look of angry determination, pages of bills he had analyzed clutched in his hand, Dad headed for the tanker truck as the driver was hooking up. He confronted the startled driver with his figures and demanded to know why he was short. The driver was baffled. He took off his cap, scratched his head and looked over Dad's figures. He knew he delivered what he billed every trip and said so, claiming he didn't understand the discrepancy. A loud argument ensued. As Dan watched from the safety of the porch he came to the realization that this was not a good thing. Angry, Dad made good on his threat to discontinue service with that company and got a different gas delivery service. That was a wake up call for Dan. He quit using so much gas, which only served to confirm Dad's suspicion that the original service had cheated him. Until today he never knew the truth.

"So what is this? Truth or consequence day?" asked Dad.

"No," said Dan. "I just thought you should know."

"Well, it's too late to do anything about it now!" said Dad.

"Yeah," laughed Dan. "You can't punish me now, but would you feel better knowing I've been punished for some things I never did?"

"Like what?"

"Like when you thought I broke all the windows out of the barn at Father's Farm."

"You didn't do that?"

No, Dan had been punished but he wasn't the one who broke every window in the lower level of the barn. This was back when Dan broke both arms falling from the apple tree. He had plaster casts on both arms, all the way up to his shoulder. He couldn't do anything for himself. He was entirely at the mercy of the rest of us.

The window incident happened when some of our 'city' cousins were visiting us on the farm. We loved these visits and spent every precious minute in some fun activity. However, with both arms broken and in casts, Dan couldn't do much but walk around. He and our cousin Joe were taking a walk around the barn when Joe noticed that one of the lower level barn windows was broken. As they walked on, Joe picked up a stick and began running down the length of the barn hitting the windows with it. Every window broke. Dan stood there in shocked amazement for a minute before he ran after Joe yelling, 'Why did you do that?' Joe replied, 'I thought it didn't matter.' The barn was old, unpainted and must have looked abandoned to Joe. They went back to the house but didn't tell anyone about the windows that day. Even when Joe's family went home that evening, Dan kept his mouth shut. He wasn't a snitch. When Father Kriskow discovered the broken windows the next day, he just assumed Dan did it with his casts and reported it to Dad, who had to pay for the repairs. No amount of talking or explaining would convince Dad that Dan was not the guilty party. After all, Father Kriskow said Dan did it and a priest would never lie or make a claim he did not know to be true. The idea that Father had just assumed Dan was guilty never occurred to Dad. So Dan was punished. When he was young he resented Dad for punishing him for something he didn't do, but as an adult he realized he was never punished for a lot of things he did do, because Dad never found out about them. And to this day Joe denies he had anything to do with the broken windows.

In our family, a broken window was one of the worst things a child could do. When Dad was young, glass was not so easy to replace and it was expensive. Dan and I experienced Dad's wrath over a broken window the year before the barn window incident. Dad had built a new house on Perry Road. Dan and I loved that house because we each had our own room. Having your own room in our family was a luxury beyond belief. My room was over the garage and Dan's was next to mine. The third bedroom upstairs was bigger and shared by the little ones: David, Rose and Gerard.

The house sat on a hill that sloped away from the street and the basement opened to the back yard. On a sunny summer afternoon we were outside playing a game we invented that combined a race, tag, and hide and seek. The basement was a safe area where you couldn't be tagged or caught. Dan was it, and I ran to the basement to escape capture. I slammed the door, locked it, and would not let Dan in. I could look out the lowest of the three windows in the door and see Dan shouting at me. Feeling pretty safe behind a locked door, I was making faces at him and laughing. In frustration, he began pounding on the door with both fists. I stood on the other side of the door, smugly playing the tormenting sister and laughing at him. He began hitting the window harder, with both fists. Suddenly, the window shattered inward and the glass fell to the floor in pieces. We both stood there, each on our own side of the door, in shocked silence. Just a minute ago we were having a great time, but now our lives had changed dramatically. We were in deep trouble. We looked at each other knowing we were as good as dead. Dad was going to kill us.

No one was hurt, but a window was broken and that meant someone was going to get it. We didn't know what to do. Mom must have been somewhere in the house where she couldn't hear what had happened. So we began to plot a cover up. Running away was an option. Where would we go? How would we live? No, running away wasn't the answer. How could we keep Dad from finding out about the window? We could live if he never found out. We couldn't fix it. And he would see it as soon as he got home from work. He parked his pickup truck in the single-car garage on one side of the basement. He could see the door as he pulled into the garage. How could you hide a broken window that was in plain sight of the driveway? We put our heads together and came up with a plan.

There was a large, tall piece of furniture in the basement. I think it was a china cabinet. Someone brought it over for Dad to repair and refinish. He didn't have time to work on it in the summer, so it had been there for a while. Our plan was simple. We opened the door with the broken window and swung it all the way open, so it was against the basement wall. Then with the strength of two scared little kids we managed to push the china cabinet in front of the open door. Success!! You couldn't see the door or that broken window. Now maybe, Dad wouldn't notice. We carefully cleaned up all the broken glass and dumped it in the trash.

As he did every day, Dad came home from work and parked in the basement garage. We watched from the back yard and breathed a sigh of relief when he closed the garage door and went upstairs. When we were called in to dinner, we both held our breath. Nothing was said about the door. As we quietly ate dinner, Dan and I exchanged worried glances. So far, so good.

Every night, before bed, Dad went around the house and made sure everything was closed up and locked for the night. This presented a new problem. What would happen when Dad checked the basement door? Dan offered to check the basement door for Dad. On the pretense of getting a toy he left down in the basement, Dan said he would check the door. Tired from working all day, Dad took Dan up on his offer. Luckily, Dad did not notice when he left for work in the morning that the basement door was open. This went on for a couple of nights, leaving the basement door open and the broken window undiscovered.

On Sunday we were going to visit our favorite cousins. Dad told all of us to pile into the car. Dan hung back and casually told Dad he would make sure everything was closed up and locked in the basement. But this time it didn't work. Dad ordered Dan to get in the car with the other kids; he would lock up himself. We sat in the car shaking. Dad was going to discover the broken window. We were dead. Maybe he wouldn't kill us on a Sunday, after church. It was our only hope. Dan sat on the floor of the car and begged us not to tell who did it.

I can still see Dad's face as he approached the car: his lips tight, face as red as a cherry, and jaw clenched shut. When he got to the car he had only one question: 'Who broke the window'? But more important than who committed this crime was: Who conspired to hide the evidence? Dan and I never felt more scared in our lives. We had to admit our guilt. I wanted to sink into the car floor and disappear. I wished to disappear, I closed my eyes tight, but when I opened them Dad was still there and just as angry. He opened the car door and invited Dan and me to follow him back to the basement for a paddling. If the good Lord had taken me right then, I would have been grateful. In my mind a paddling was the worst thing that could happen. I never got paddled. The boys were the ones always in trouble. But in spite of my fervent prayers, I remained on this earth. After the paddling, I realized the punishment actually wasn't so bad. And now that the truth was out, the constant fear of being found out was gone. I learned a lesson that day. It's better to admit a wrong than compound it with a cover up. I really doubt if Dan learned the same lesson; through the years he continued to get in trouble and try to hide his misdeeds.

For some reason, after that incident Dad was a little more tolerant of broken windows. That was probably Mom's doing. With so many kids, broken windows are a common occurrence. We were never that afraid to admit we broke a window again.

As the laughter subsides from the window story, Dan asks Dad if he remembers the McDonald's fry wrapper incident. With a smile, Dad says of course he does. Thankfully, he can laugh about it now. It wasn't so funny then.

When Dan was 15 years old, he had the typical teenage boy's desire to drive a car. However, in Ohio at that time, you had to be 16 to get your learner's permit. Like many farm boys, Dan had been driving tractors and trucks on the farm since his legs could reach the gas and brake pedals. He was an experienced driver at 15. Now he was looking for an opportunity to get behind the wheel of a car on a real road.

Mom and Dad treated themselves to a night out on Fridays. They joined a bowling league. As usual, I was the resident babysitter. Dan knew exactly when they would be home each Friday and decided he would borrow Dad's car. As soon as they left, he took Dad's old station wagon and drove to McDonald's where his friends hung out. Being cool, he drove in a circle around the restaurant, like everyone else in his crowd. They were already 16. No one realized he didn't have a license. He drove the car home, got it back in the garage, and would be sitting in front of the TV when Mom and Dad got home. This worked well for Dan all of that autumn.

Each week David begged to tag along. He was 13 and wanted to be as cool as his older brother. Besides, trips to McDonald's were rare, and he loved fries and a milkshake. Dan wouldn't take him along; having your little brother with you was not cool. But finally, David threatened to break the sibling code of silence and tell Dad what Dan had been up to, if he didn't take him. Dan wasn't sure David would actually break the code; breaking it could result in some miserable weeks of torture from the rest of us, but Dan felt he couldn't take that chance. So, he took David with him. David loved it. He ate McDonald's fries and rode around with his brother like a cool guy. Dan returned the car before Mom and Dad got home and was innocently watching TV when they walked into the house.

The next morning, Dad kissed Mom goodbye and left for work as usual, as Dan was eating his breakfast. Dan looked out the kitchen window as he finished his cereal, only to see Dad walking back to the house. Dan could almost see the steam rising from Dad's head as he marched toward the house with a McDonald's fry wrapper clenched in his fist. Dan realized there was no use running; he had been caught. To this day Dan has not forgiven David for the French fry wrapper incident.

Dan came close to getting caught a few weeks before that. One night after an evening of being cool, driving around the local McDonald's, he was returning the car to its space in the garage when the clutch went out. Now he was in trouble. In a panic, he got David to help push the car into the garage. Then he and David got under the car and fixed the clutch so that, hopefully when Dad backed it out of the garage on Saturday he would think it had just happened.

The next morning at breakfast Dan sat at the table trying to act natural, as if nothing was going to happen when Dad tried to leave for work. Dad kissed Mom goodbye, headed for the door and waved to the kids at the table. Dan held his breath while Dad backed the old station wagon out of the garage. Dan watched as Dad attempted to shift to drive unsuccessfully. As Dan watched, Dad got out of the car and headed for the house. He looked mad. Did he somehow know Dan did it? Was Dan in real trouble again? Dad came through the door complaining about that 'old car' and telling Mom the clutch went out on him. He would need to take the good car to work. Dan breathed a sigh of relief knowing he dodged another one. However, this close call still did not deter Dan from his regular Friday night drive the next weekend.

Dad sat there in the hospital cafeteria just shaking his head as the younger boys laughed at Dan's story. Right now those old transgressions seem trivial. Dad realized Dan had not been so different than he had been at that age. Dad had many stories of stunts he pulled as a boy. However, he was not in a mood to share them now. Right now all he had on his mind was Mom and her recovery.

# Chapter Seven

## *Water fights*

As we settle back in the waiting room our conversation turns yet again to growing up. As each of us waits our turn to see Mom, we fill the hours reminiscing about the times we spent together as a family. The good news from the doctors on Mom's progress has everyone in a much better frame of mind. Conversations get a little loud at times. Occasionally a nurse sticks her head in the door and asks us to quiet down. Our better mood is causing us to forget where we are. It is so good to have some time to share with each other again. But we recall times growing up, when we were pretty rough with each other.

After Nancy passed away, there was no need to spend winters in Florida. We settled into a less nomadic life. Although they missed their beautiful little girl, Mom and Dad no longer had the worry and constant medical bills for Nancy.

We lived in the city when Nancy passed away, but Dad's heart was in the country. He decided to build a new home for his wife and five remaining children. He picked a nice spot outside of Canton on the side of a hill surrounded by farmland. He did most of the work on the new house himself. Some of our relatives helped Dad in trade for carpenter work. Dad worked on the house on weekends and in the evening, after his regular eight-hour workday for a local contractor. We accompanied him, playing on the huge piles of dirt and running through the unfinished house. Mom took dinner to Dad on nights when he went directly from work to the new house.

When the house was finished we were excited to move in. It was early summer and I had just completed the second grade. The new house seemed so open after living in the city where the houses were built right next to each other. We had a huge yard to play in and Dan and I had our own rooms. Before that we had all shared a room, with bunk beds. There was one bedroom down and three upstairs. Mom and Dad had the downstairs bedroom. My bedroom was small, over the single-car garage, but it was mine. I was eight years old and had never had my own space before. Dan, who would turn seven in July, had the room next to mine. The third bedroom upstairs was large and had plenty of room for five year-old David, Rosemary who would be four in August, and the baby, Gerard. Marie was born while we lived there. We would be going to a new school in the fall. Everything was new and fresh. I loved to gaze out of the two big picture windows in the front of the house at the barn across the street and watch the horses running in the pasture.

Mom loved the house Dad had built for us and wanted to take good care of it. But we did not always make that easy for her. Dan and I remember the first water fight we had. It was in that nice new house.

Mom took the rest of the kids to pick up a few things at the store, less than two miles away. Dan and I stayed home, with instructions to do the lunch dishes. As I washed the baby bottles and nipples I discovered I could get a pretty good stream of water going by filling a nipple with water and pressing my thumb into it. I surprised Dan with a squirt in the face. He retaliated by pulling the vegetable sprayer out of the sink and soaking me. I ran to the bathroom around the corner to elude him, but every time I came back around the corner he got me with the sprayer. Without thinking, I grabbed a glass and started throwing glasses full of water his way. The battle was in full swing when Mom appeared at the kitchen door, Gerard in one arm and a grocery bag in the other, followed closely by Rose and David. It was a hot summer day and she was seven months pregnant with Marie. Mom's hair was sticking to her forehead and she looked exhausted. When I looked at her I saw an expression of shock, quickly followed by angry disappointment.

That's when I realized that most of the water had not hit the targets. I watched Mom's eyes sweep over the devastation. Water was running across the floor, down the walls, the counter and cabinets. The new curtains, which Mom had just carefully hung at the kitchen window, were dripping. Water had even flowed into the dining room onto the hardwood floor. Mom ordered us to get rags and the mop. We spent the afternoon helping her dry everything off. Mom was so mad she didn't even talk to us as we worked. Dan and I silently worried about Dad's reaction when he saw what we had done to his beautiful new kitchen. We stole quick glances at each other as we worked. I prayed to God all afternoon that he would spare me the spanking and I would never do anything wrong again as long as I lived. While I survived the spanking, and the kitchen was not permanently damaged, I never participated in a water fight again.

Water fights were sometimes the best way to keep cool in the summer. Many of the kids waged war with squirt guns, buckets and hoses out in the yard every July and August. Mom usually kept a watchful eye on her kids running and squealing with delight as they soaked each other on hot afternoons. As the kids got older the water fights got bigger. Many years later, when we had moved to Louisville, the older kids let a water fight get a little out of hand. It was a particularly hot summer afternoon and the water battle was raging in the back yard. There were more kids at the time and David was old enough to be the babysitter while Mom ran some errands. Marie was getting the best of Vince, but when he got his hands on the water hose, it was payback time. Marie ran to the back door and took refuge in the kitchen. Figuring she was safe, she walked to the open window to taunt Vince. A blast of water came right through the screen and sent her reeling backwards across the kitchen. By the time Vince stopped the flow of water, everything in the kitchen was drenched. Water was a half-inch deep on the floor.

When they realized what Vince had done, everybody grabbed towels and started mopping up. But they weren't fast enough. Mom came up the drive before they were finished, catching them in the cover-up. She was furious, mostly at David whom she had left in charge. She gave quite a lecture on water fights not being an indoor activity.

Water was not the only weapon used in the wars of the Johanning kids. In the winter we produced snowballs in mass amount and stored them in snow forts. We called a truce whenever anyone needed to restock his or her fort, and battles never started until everyone was ready. After all, the fun was in the battle, not the victory.

The afternoon flies by as different siblings come in and out of the waiting room, talking and sharing memories. We've all had a chance to see Mom and it's time to say goodnight and get some rest. We leave for homes or hotel rooms in the hope of a restful night. We're sure tomorrow Mom will be even better, and some of us need to think about getting back to Ohio, to jobs and families. As I leave the hospital with my daughters, I can't help noticing what a beautiful evening it is. So warm and quiet, with just the slightest breeze and a carpet of stars in the sky. I wonder how everything can appear so normal outside the hospital. Everyone is going about their business, restaurants are full of people enjoying dinner, there are shoppers in the stores, and children are playing in their yards. Mom is one of the most important people in my life, and I feel so powerless to help her. Will Mom be all right? Will her life go back to normal? Will things ever be the same? Tired and worried, I start the car and drive to the motel, praying for some answers. That's the only place I can find the answers, in prayers. That's what Mom taught me.

# Chapter Eight

## *Raised Catholic*

The next morning at the hospital, we meet the priest from Mom and Dad's church, St. Elizabeth Sedan in Naples. Father Joe visits Mom every day. She takes great comfort in praying with him. I admire her deep faith as I watch her chatting with Father Joe. She is so comforted by his presence. As I remember my years of Catholic education and regular worship, I am comforted too.

Mom is a devout believer in prayer and spends many hours with her rosary. The repetition of the familiar prayers and the faith that God is listening helped Mom through many hard times. The Church played a major part in my parents' ability to raise such a large family. They believe that God provides for those who work to provide for themselves. Even though they needed their money to feed and clothe the large family God blessed them with, they always gave as generously as they could to the church.

For years our family said the rosary together, every evening after dinner. As soon as the news ended, Dad turned off the TV and called us all together. We knelt beside chairs and tables around the living room, and Dad led us in prayer. We each had a rosary of our own. But Dad's was our favorite. His rosary glows in the dark with beads as large as grapes. Each of the cream colored beads is carved with a religious picture. It always hung in the family room or living room, draped over our picture of Jesus and the Apostles at 'The Last Supper.' If, during the night, we went to the bathroom in the dark, the rosary glowed reassuringly against the wall. As we got older and started dating we continued to say the rosary nearly every night. If our dates were at the house at rosary time, they were expected to join us, Catholic or not. Dating a 'non-Catholic' was frowned upon. Mom and Dad envisioned all of their children either having a vocation to the Church or marrying a Catholic boy or girl and raising a big Catholic family.

We complained. There are five sets of 10 repetitions of 'Hail Mary's' with the Lord's Prayer between each set. It starts and ends with the 'Sign of the Cross,' with the Apostle's Creed near the beginning. By the time we finished saying the rosary, our knees hurt from kneeling on the floor for 10 to 15 minutes. Sometimes we tried to rush through the prayers as quickly as we could so we could watch a favorite TV show or go out with friends. It never worked. Dad made us say the rosary again if our prayers were not heartfelt the first time. No one wanted to be the cause of a second round of prayers, so we were a devout group of angels, if only for 10 to 15 minutes.

We attended Mass every Sunday. The older kids loved St. Mary's Church in Morges. Morges is so small it consists of only the church and a cluster of houses. St. Mary's church sits on the top of a picturesque hill, overlooking rolling farmland in Carroll County, Ohio. The building is tiny compared to St. Peter's in Canton. Dad did quite a bit of carpentry work for the church. The kids went along and played for hours in the church cemetery. We loved to play tag among the headstones. Many of the grave markers were so windblown we could no longer make out the names or dates. Others told of mysterious deaths, and many dates spoke of very short lives. We spent hours imagining what the people had been like and what they did while they were alive.

The church had a social hall that had just been completed when we moved to the area. The congregation held fundraisers in the hall to help pay the mortgage. My favorite fundraisers were the 'nickel dinners' held after the 10 a.m. Mass, one Sunday each month. Each item on the menu cost a nickel, enabling guests to eat a complete meal for a quarter. The parishioners donated most of the food. Along with the other ladies in the congregation, Mom always cooked and baked for the dinners. On Saturday the men set up the tables and chairs in the basement of the hall. The young girls in the parish were servers, and the ladies prepared the food. Everyone helped with cleanup. The hall would be full of families, occupying every table. Neighbors and friends could catch up on the latest news, sharing crop forecasts, current milk prices, and livestock costs from the local auctions. It was a joyful party for everyone, whether eating or working.

Bingo night also helped pay off the mortgage. Dad loved to run bingo night each week. We held square dances to raise money, too. Mom and Dad loved square dancing. Dad would twirl Mom around the floor, her full colorful skirt flying around her legs. They could forget their troubles and just enjoy the music and each other for the evening. They tried to raise money with a teen's square dance night. That was not very successful. The adults didn't understand it just wasn't cool to square dance in the 1950s. Rock and roll was the new thing. We watched 'Bandstand' after school, and you would never catch the cool kids square dancing.

Holidays at the church were exciting, too. The Christmas party for the kids was always a big hit. There wasn't much money for decorations, but there was a tree in the corner and white paper snowflakes hanging from the ceiling. Every child received red mesh stockings with small toys and treats in them. Someone would read the story of the first Christmas as the children sat around in a circle on the floor. The night was topped off with Christmas cookies baked by our Moms, and red punch served from a big glass punch bowl.

The annual Halloween party introduced us to bobbing for apples and other ghoulish games. That was one night we didn't play in the cemetery. It was scary just walking past it to get to the car.

St. Mary's had a small group of Altar Boys who assisted the priest with Mass. As an altar boy, Dan often served both Masses on Sunday. We went to early Mass so Dan could serve, then he stayed at the Leggett's house, next door to the church for breakfast, and serve the second Mass. Then Dad picked him up before dinner.

Every Sunday, Dad was responsible for ringing the church bell to signal that Mass was about to begin. One Sunday as he was pulling on the bell pull, it got stuck straight upside down. No amount of pulling on the rope would move it. Now we didn't have a bell to ring when Sunday Mass was starting. The parishioners missed the beautiful sound of the bell calling them to Sunday service. Dad volunteered to fix it. He didn't relish the idea of climbing up into the small, hot belfry. But he took a deep breath at the bottom and started climbing up into the narrow tower. When he got to the top there was very little room to work. As he tried to loosen the bell, Father Bernie stood at the bottom of the tower shouting encouragement. The bell refused to budge. Sweat rolled down Dad's face as he tried to maneuver the pulley in the tight space. It seemed to him the area he had to work in grew hotter and smaller as each minute ticked by. He stretched as far as he could to get a grip on the bell itself. He leaned into it, balancing his weight on his thigh, against the pulley, where the rope circled it. Gripping the bell and pulling with all the strength he could muster, Dad swung the bell around to its down position. At the same time, the sheave's sharp edge sliced through his work pants and deep into his thigh. He looked down to see an open wound through the clean cut in his pants and felt blood running down his leg. After the initial shock passed, he felt the pain. As he looked down he wondered: how could he get down with a painful gaping slash in his leg? No one could fit in the small space with him to help. He had no choice; he climbed down, with the fresh wound bleeding.

Father Bernie was waiting at the bottom of the belfry ladder as Dad descended. When he saw Dad's leg and all the blood, he panicked. He helped Dad to the car intending to rush him to the hospital. As Dad reached for the door handle on the passenger side, he looked over the roof of the car at Father Bernie, standing near the driver's door. Father was ghostly pale and obviously in no condition to drive a car. He looked like he was about to pass out. Dad said, "Maybe I should drive." Father Bernie nodded as Dad limped to the driver's door. Dad kept up a constant chatter to calm Father Bernie. Dad was sure Father Bernie would pass out any moment. It took a lot of stitches to close the wound, but it eventually healed. And the church had the morning service bell again.

Father Bernie was in absolute awe of our family. He often came to the farm for Sunday dinners. He loved the noise and confusion. He was from the city, and farm life fascinated him. When he learned we raised our own cattle for beef and butchered the steers and cut up and froze our meat, he wanted to see how it was done. He had eaten beef all his life but never thought about where it came from. He arrived on a cool fall morning to witness the first phase of butchering, killing the steer. After watching that process, he insisted he would never eat meat again. He had been blissfully unaware of how the juicy roast beef and delightful steaks he enjoyed were produced. But two weeks later he was back at our table for Sunday dinner with a big steak on his plate. Apparently his love of meat overcame his squeamishness.

In time, Father Bernie seemed to become a part of the family. My parents so loved Father Bernie they named their fifth son after him. That was as close as they would come to having a child enter the priesthood. My parents believed giving a child to the church to serve as a priest, nun, or brother would be wonderful. We had relatives who were priests and nuns, and Mom and Dad were sure one of their children would be called to the church. Even when Dan and I were very small, Mom and Dad talked about one of us being that special one. After all, they believed giving a child to serve to the church assures your entry into heaven.

When I was in grade school, I walked around the house with a blue towel over my head, pretending to be a nun. Some of my sisters did the same thing. At one time I believed I was the one that would be called, but as I got older I realized I wanted a husband and family, like my parents. I

70

couldn't imagine spending my life any way other than how I grew up. Family was just too important and having children of my own meant everything to me. I envisioned the life of a nun as very lonely. Having so many sisters and brothers, the idea of being alone didn't appeal to me. That ended any hope my parents had for me.

Dan was the next possibility. After all, he was an altar boy and looked just like an angel up at the altar serving Mass on Sunday. Nothing like at home. There was hope that Dan would be the chosen one. Dan's grades were not good enough to study for the priesthood, however. But locally we had a high school for boys who wanted to be a brother, a vocation similar to the role of the nun. Brothers teach or work in hospitals but they are not priests. My parents asked Dan if he would like to go to Brunnerdale Seminary, the school for Brothers, instead of Central Catholic, where I attended high school. Dan was excited and said he'd like to go.

One beautiful Sunday afternoon we joined others at a picnic for families who were considering enrolling a boy in the school. The centerpiece of the Brunnerdale campus was a majestic building, with a lake in front. Dan took a tour of the school guided by students, as we waited on the manicured lawn. Brunnerdale was a boarding school, and Dan would live in a dorm with the other boys. The students told him about all the fun they had, playing outdoor games, working together on the school farm, and fishing on the lake. Dan was excited about going to school there, and Dad signed him up for his freshman year. The cost was high, but this was important enough that they would find a way to pay for it. Dan had a vocation, and Mom and Dad would make sure he could serve the church. When September came, we accompanied Dan to the seminary. There were tearful goodbyes all around, but we knew this was a good thing for Dan.

No one realized Dan only went because it made Mom and Dad happy. At the school he was miserable. He was homesick. There were plenty of other boys there, but they weren't his brothers and sisters. We were not permitted to visit him for the first few months, and he missed us so much he was actually sick. We were not even allowed to communicate with him by phone. So we wrote letters, but that didn't make up for what he was missing at home.

The fun he was told about on the tour didn't materialize. In addition to the schoolwork, there was plenty of farm work, and Dan had a lot of chores. Since he had experience driving tractors he usually got that job, which he enjoyed. But that didn't make up for how homesick he felt. He really wanted to be back in a regular school with friends and family.

Finally, Thanksgiving weekend arrived and the boys were permitted to visit home. Dan was sort of a celebrity in our house now, a 14 year-old holy man. We were taught to respect priests, nuns and brothers, so there was almost a reverence in our feelings about seeing Dan. But when he came through the door, he looked just like Dan. There was no halo, no difference in his manner, just the Dan we always knew.

We enjoyed dinner, and later in the afternoon Dan asked me if we could talk in private. We went up to my bedroom. Dan shocked me with his announcement. He was not going back to Brunnerdale. "You have to!" I exclaimed. "Dad will kill you!"

"I just can't go back," He said. "I hate it! You've got to help me!"

I sat on my bed telling him how proud Dad was of him and why he had to go back. But he wouldn't listen. When he asked me, "Would you go, if you were me?" I had to admit, I wouldn't.

He begged me to tell Dad for him, because Dad wouldn't do anything to me. But I was not about to get in the middle of this. After Dan begged and begged I went to Dad and told him, 'Dan has something to tell you.' Dan was so scared he wouldn't unlock my bedroom door. He talked through the door. Dad tried to tell him he would feel better in time and to give it another chance. But it didn't take long for Dad to realize that Dan was right. He didn't make him return to the seminary. After it was all over we were glad to have Dan back with us, even if he was always getting the rest of the kids in some kind of trouble.

Marie appeared to be good candidate for a vocation. After all, she was a special gift from God. She was so like Nancy there must have been a special reason God gave her to us. But again Mom and Dad were disappointed when Marie showed no interest. As we grew, they talked to different kids about a vocation in the church, but their heart was no longer in it. Apparently this was not a gift they could give to the Church.

Being faithful Catholics we went to Church every Sunday. At Mass some Sundays, Dad had a problem with the sermon. If the church was warm and the sermon long, Dad often nodded off. Mom sat at one end of the pew and Dad at the other. If Dad nodded off, Mom would pass the word down the row to nudge Dad and wake him up, before he started snoring. We all hated to sit next to Dad and have to elbow him awake.

My parents taught us respect for the clergy. So much so, that sweet little Gerard got confused. I remember the Sunday Father Bernie really got into his sermon, getting rather loud and forceful on the subject of sin and sinners. Gerard, about 6 years old at the time, sat beside Mom in the front pew. The longer he sat there watching Father Bernie, the more frightened he became. When he couldn't take it any more he let out with a howl, tears streaming down his face. Mom quietly got up and walked him down the center aisle, and out the door as we all turned to watch them go. Surely he was in some kind of pain. When any of us cry, we are not quiet about it. Some people can quietly cry or allow tears to silently run down their cheeks. In my family, we wail. Mom was sure this wailing meant something awful. But, his response to her worried questions was a surprise: "God is yelling at me." Relieved, Mom explained, Father Bernie wasn't yelling at him, he was just talking loudly for emphasis. Father Bernie would never yell at him because he was a good boy in church. Gerard returned to the pew without further incident, but sat there wide-eyed for the rest of the service.

After Mass we often chatted with Father Bernie in the parking lot before leaving for home. That Sunday, as the car moved toward the road, little Gerard leaned out of the car window waving to Father Bernie and shouted, "Bye, God." That's when we realized; Gerard thought Father Bernie was God.

We often invited the priests from the churches we attended through the years to Sunday dinner. The kids loved Father Martin. He usually came to dinner on Sundays. He would do magic tricks to entertain the little ones and allowed the kids to climb all over him, as if he were a jungle gym. The kids ran out to meet him as he pulled up in his car. In the driveway Father Martin would perform his favorite trick. Sitting in the driver's seat, he raised both hands above his head and commanded the headlights to come on, and then go off. The little kids were amazed. They had no idea the headlights were controlled by a button of the floor of the car.

Whenever possible, we attended Catholic school. A Catholic education was important to my parents. Like most of the kids in school, we were afraid of the nuns. And if we had any problem at school, Mom and Dad usually sided with the nuns. If sister punished us, and Mom and Dad found out, we were punished again. There was one exception. I am left-handed, like Dad. When I was in the third grade the teacher insisted I use my right hand. My right hand was just about useless; I did everything with my left. My teacher was further infuriated by my name. Kathy! That is not a saint's name. She believed everyone must be named after a saint. Using a pagan name was unheard of. I often wondered how there would ever be any new saint's names if everyone were required to use only names of current saints? Anyway, she required me to put Catherine or Kathleen on all my papers. I could not learn how to spell either name correctly. Every time I spelled the name wrong on a paper my grade was lowered. My grades weren't that good to start with, so this was a problem.

Every time she caught me writing with my left hand she smacked it with the metal edge of her ruler. After a while my left hand was pretty beat up. But my right hand just would not do what I wanted it to do on the paper. Anything I wrote with my right hand wasn't legible, so I still got a bad grade. I came home from school crying many days with my low grades on assignments written with my right hand.

Finally Mom confronted the nun and made her stop. That was not easy for her to do. She was taught respect for the nuns and everything they did was to be accepted. But one of her children was not in the wrong this time and she worked up the courage to confront a nun to correct the problem. I was grateful.

Some of us had Sister Marie as a teacher at St. Louis. Sister Marie Rosaire could pick you up, right out of your chair, by your cheek. My rambunctious brothers gave her plenty of exercise, pulling them out of their seats by the cheek. If the boys complained to Mom she said; "You probably deserved it. Behave in class and that won't happen." There was absolutely no sympathy at home. We all thought the nuns didn't like us, so we stayed out of their way.

On special Holy Days and during Lent, Mass was offered before the school day started. If we went to communion, we ate our breakfast at school. They served a little box of cereal and milk. We thought that was great; at home Mom never bought the individual boxes of cereal. They were way too expensive and she said there was nothing in them. So we went to communion often, but not necessarily for the right reasons.

Since we moved so many times, I went to five different grade schools. I started with St. Peter's grade school in downtown Canton. That was when Nancy was still alive, and moving back and forth from Florida meant Dad couldn't have a farm. He settled for the city. I spent two years there. After Nancy was gone, Dad built the new house on Perry Road, and I spent a year at St. Joan of Arc in Perry Township. My memories of that school are; a sore left hand, always missing the bus because I could never remember my bus number and getting the mumps.

After Dad sold the house and moved to Father's farm, we attended Sacred Heart of Jesus parish in Canton. The school was a two-room building with four grades in each room. Dan, David and I went to that building and Rose was in kindergarten, held in a house the parish owned across the street. There were four rows of desks in each room, and each grade level occupied one row. Two nuns taught in the school, one for each room. Sister would stand in front of the row of seats with the grade she was teaching at that moment. The rest of us had assignments to do until it was our turn. We learned a lot from listening to the older kids do their lessons.

While we attended the two-room school, the state of Ohio changed the law, and no more the two grades were permitted to share a classroom. That meant the school had to cut down to four grades. David and Rose had to go to St. Benedict's. There was nothing wrong with St. Benedict's school, except David and Rose were no longer going to school with Dan and me. We didn't like separation. It didn't last long, because Dad scraped together the money to buy a farm in Carroll County, where there were no Catholic schools. We attended a public school in nearby New Harrisburg, a tiny country town with a gas station, school, church, small store and the Grange Hall. But the school had four rooms, with two classes per room and a real gym. On our first day, we were shocked to find there was no indoor plumbing for bathrooms. The only plumbing in the building was for a small kitchen where two ladies cooked lunch. Out back there were two small buildings, located at each rear corner of the school's three-acre property. One was marked boys and the other girls. If we needed to use the bathroom during class we raised our hand, with our finger pointing to the door and the teacher would nod if we were permitted to go.

This was our first experience with teachers who were not nuns. And not only were the teachers not nuns, we were the only Catholic kids in the whole school.  Suddenly being Catholic made us different, something we had never experienced.

But our Catholic education continued with Saturday Catechism classes.  Every Saturday during the school year, we went to St. Mary's for religious education by the nuns.  We just couldn't escape them.

On Saturday Dad marched the older kids to church for Confession.  We were sinners who had to confess so we could take Communion the next day.  If we didn't take Communion on Sunday, Dad wanted to know just what we had done that would prevent us from taking Communion.  Apparently it was a pretty nasty sin and we were in big trouble.  So we confessed every Saturday.  But we were actually pretty good kids.  There wasn't much to tell the priest.  We did what we were told most of the time.  Most of the trouble we got into was really pretty mild.  So, what was there to confess?  Not much.  We got really good at making up sins on Saturday.

We went into the confessional, devoutly knelt and stated, as taught, "Forgive me Father for I have sinned. My last confession was a week ago."  Wow, a whole week of sinning.  This should be good.  We had a practiced litany of sins we used every week: talked back to my mother three times (I was scared to death to talk back to Mom), hit my brothers and sisters six times (that sounds cruel), I took the Lord's name if vain five times (Yeah, and get my mouth washed out with soap, I don't think so).  But this was our regular list of sins.  It didn't pay to get too fancy.  Dan once confessed to looking at dirty pictures.  The priest wanted to know where he got the pictures and what they were.  Since the sin he just confessed was not true and he didn't know what a dirty picture was, Dan didn't have an answer.

After our list of lies (Oh yeah! there's a sin), we would hear our penance and say our Act of Contrition.  Then we would do penance for sins we never committed.  I like to think those penance prayers went into the bank to cover sins committed later, as we got older.

As we became teenagers church lost its appeal for many of us, especially the boys. By this time we moved to Louisville and attended St. Louis. Compared to St. Mary's in Morges, which had about 10 rows of pews on each side of the main aisle, this church was a cathedral. They had five Masses each Sunday. When the boys were old enough to drive a car, they chose a Mass that neither Mom nor Dad was attending. They drove to church, ran in the door and grabbed a bulletin as proof they had been to church. They spent the hour at a friend's house or drove around town. After Mass was over they would show up at home, announcing they had picked up the bulletin in case Mom and Dad had forgotten one. That was not a lie. They did pick up a bulletin; they just didn't mention they didn't stay for Mass.

The Catholic Church has many services in addition to the regular Sunday Mass. Dad attended these services and took the kids with him. During Lent we attended the Stations of the Cross on Friday evenings. The priest went from station to station, which depicted an aspect of the last days of the life of Christ, and prayed at each with the congregation joining in. As the kids got older, they resisted since on Friday night they wanted to go out with friends. We were required to attend Mass on Sunday, but as we got older other services were by choice. Dad resorted to bribery to get us to accompany him. If we went to the Stations of the Cross he would take us somewhere special, like the local drug store soda fountain for a root beer float. That provided him with some company at the Stations of the Cross.

Moving to Louisville meant we could go to Catholic school again. One of the things Mom loved (and we hated) about Catholic school was the uniform. With a uniform Mom didn't have to spend a lot of money keeping up with the latest fashions for school. The girl's uniform was a dark blue polyester jumper with a white blouse and saddle shoes. The boys were dressed in light blue shirts, dark blue pants and blue ties. That made school clothes shopping much easier, even with that many kids to dress.

To enroll their children in Catholic school Mom and Dad had to pay tuition. With so many in the school it got more expensive every year. Large families got a price break depending on the number of kids enrolled in the school. Catholic high school was much more expensive than grade school. I was first to attend high school. My parents asked me if I wanted to attend Central Catholic High School in Canton. It would be a sacrifice but if I wanted to attend they would send me. I was shy and being new in Louisville I had not made a lot of friends in the one year I attended St Louis. Going to a school out of town would be a fresh start for me and I was eager to go. So I was enrolled at Central. We wore uniforms, this time a plaid skirt and blue blazer. (Much better.) We had to buy all my books; the school did not provide them. It was expensive but with babysitting and part time jobs I could help out. Dan, on the other hand, had tried Brunnerdale Seminary and that didn't work out. With so many kids going to St. Louis grade school, the cost of sending everyone to Central Catholic High School would be too much. Mom and Dad decided the public school system would have to do and the rest of the kids attended the local public high school.

With such a large family, college was not an option my parents could offer their children. They both considered us a working class family and believed in preparing the boys for jobs such as carpenter work and the girls to be good mothers and wives. The opportunity for education stopped when we graduated from high school. The kids could have gone on to college on their own, but we were all more interested in getting jobs and starting families.

As we talk with Father outside Mom's room, I am reminded of my parents' deep faith and I know faith will sustain them, whatever happens to Mom. They believe that with the help of God, they can get through anything. Knowing of their faith helps me relax and realize Mom's recovery is out of my hands. Prayer and patience will have to be my role. Understanding that, I feel myself relax a little.

# Chapter Nine

## *Animals*

We gather at Dad's house in the evening and are enthusiastically greeted by the current family pet, a black and white, long hair, mixed breed dog. Like most of the dogs we owned as a family he is a mutt. Mom calls every dog a mutt and was never fond of any of the dogs we collected. Yet here is another one, greeting us with wildly wagging tail and drooling tongue, as if we are his long lost family. Visit my parents' house anytime and a friendly animal will greet you.

Pets were a fixture around the farm and house. Mom and Dad were not exceptionally fond of animals, but with that many children the pet parade was inevitable. When a kid arrived home with yet another cat or dog, they would insist that the animal followed them, even though they made every effort to discourage it. That could only mean they were meant to be together. How could Mom deny destiny? Mom would say, "Don't feed it and it will go home, where it belongs." Most of these animals however, were strays and didn't have a home to go back to.

The kids would sneak food to the newcomer and make sure it was closed into the garage or any available building for the night just in case it might consider leaving. After a few days the new pet would become a part of the family and be given the reluctant nod by Mom, as she stated, "you're going to take care of it." Most of our pets were adopted that way. When she got tired of the pet, Mom was not above sneaking an animal off to the pound when the kids were at school and insisting she had no idea what happened to it. She told them, as they called for the animal, it probably went home to its family, many miles away, like the Disney stories. For many years the kids were none the wiser.

Mom didn't care for dogs and cats but she loved kittens and puppies. As animals matured she tired of them easily. But if a cat had kittens she cared for the cat and played endlessly with the kittens. A litter was once produced in the laundry room off the kitchen. Mom always acted as if she wasn't interested in the new litter of kittens but we could sneak up on her and catch her playing with the kittens when no one was watching.

David was the rescuer of homeless or injured animals. He took in any animal and nursed it back to health. On the farm, he was the one who rescued the runt of the litter of pigs. Animals were his thing. He made pets of any animal he could, even one of the chickens that had a bad leg. His chicken followed him around the farm, often sitting on his shoulder or his head. He named her "Popeye." Popeye came to an untimely end when she toppled off the wrong side of a fence and landed in the pigpen. Being unable to move fast, David's beloved chicken became a delicious meal for a couple of large, nasty hogs. David has never forgiven the porcine community for this transgression.

Marie, on the other hand, hated chickens. We had a couple of ill-tempered roosters on the farm. One day Marie was walking near the barn when a rooster took a disliking to her and attacked. Shocked, Marie fell flat on her back, screaming. The rooster was on top of her, flapping its wings and making all sorts of noises. Marie was screaming so loudly you could hear her all the way to the house. The more she screamed the more the rooster flapped his wings. The boys came running and she was rescued before any real damage was done. Marie was fine physically but what a traumatic experience for a three year old. The rooster however, did not find the court of Mom and Dad very forgiving. He was sentenced to death for his crime of traumatizing a little girl, and made a delicious chicken noodle soup. To this day we tease Marie about her chicken phobia.

Gerard, a gentle little guy, was another kid with a love of animals. His job as a small boy on the farm was to feed chickens and gather eggs. Being in charge of poultry meant he had to care for the new peeps that would someday be laying hens. They were fragile but such fun to play with. To his despair he accidentally killed two of them when he dropped a brooder lamp he was adjusting. The brooder lamp was used to keep the little peeps warm in the absence of a mother hen. Besides being devastated at the loss of the peeps, he was sure he was in big trouble with Dad. So he went to his big brother David for help.

There were hundreds of baby peeps, so many we couldn't keep track of them. Dad would never know any were missing. So David helped Gerard plan a cover up. They would sneak out when Dad was busy with barn work and bury the peeps. They found a spot in the pasture, not too near the barn and hurriedly covered up the evidence. Being small and not wise in the ways of the wild they didn't bury them well enough. The next thing they knew something had uncovered the evidence. They saw the downy feathers of the unfortunate peeps exposed near the tiny grave in the pasture. There was no time to hide the exposed evidence before Dad happened by. They waited wide-eyed, behind the gate, watching as Dad approached. He walked right by the exhumed remains of the two baby chicks. He didn't even notice. The boys let out a simultaneous sigh of relief as Dad walked around the corner without stopping. Another unfortunate accident would go undetected and unpunished.

We had a couple of ducks, too. Those also fell under Gerard's jurisdiction. It didn't take him long to turn them into his special pets. After a very short time he had them trained. He felt all ducks were entitled to have duck-style fun. That meant swimming and playing in the water. But there was no water near the barn for them to swim in. Gerard decided the creek down the road would be an ideal spot for ducks to enjoy an afternoon of swimming. But he needed a safe way to transport the ducks to and from the creek. So, he built a crate just the right size to hold two ducks. He taught them to walk over to the crate, which he laid on its side. When Gerard whistled, the ducks waddled into the crate and Gerard loaded it into his cherished red wagon. With an old piece of twine, he tied the wagon to his bike and pulled the ducks down the road to the creek for an afternoon swim.

After they had a good long swim and Gerard took a nap on the banks of the creek, he whistled and the ducks waddled up on shore and back into the crate. He'd load them into his wagon again, and pedal home. But then we got out of the chicken and egg business and sold all the poultry to another farmer. The ducks went with the chickens. As far as Dad was concerned, animals were a business, not pets.

Cats were a regular fixture around the barn and Dad said ours were working cats. They were there to keep mice and rats away. He discouraged feeding them, saying it made them lazy and not good mousers. In spite of Dad's 'no feeding' policy we would catch him breaking his own rules. If we snuck up on Dad as he was milking the cows, we saw a row of cats lined up near him. A little spying on Dad soon explained the phenomenon. As he milked the cow he occasionally squirted a little milk at the line of cats. They were all waiting patiently for that warm mouthful of fresh milk.

My brothers played a little rough with the cats. They loved to toss cats on the tin roof of a low shed and watch them slide down and over the edge where a kid would catch them. The cats tried to hold on with their claws, but there was nothing for their claws to grip on the smooth metal roof. Thankfully, it was a low roof and the boys were there to catch the cats. One time Dad was working on the other side of a shed where a couple of boys were tossing a cat. One of the boys tossed a little high and the cat landed on the crown of the roof. As the boys watched, the cat teetered on the top the roof and then slid down the other side. It landed right on Dad's back as he was stooped over working. Dad let out a holler that sent the cat running into the bushes. The boys tossing the cat did not get to enjoy the sight. Dad yelled over the shed and those boys scrambled and disappeared in a matter of seconds. That ended the cat tossing.

Dad's patience wore thin with many of our pets, like the rabbits. With Dad's help the boys built hutches beside the barn and tried their hand at raising rabbits. Occasionally someone would leave the cage door open after feeding the rabbits or cleaning the cages. One Sunday morning as we were leaving for church we discovered the rabbits were out and hopping everywhere. We couldn't leave while they were out; the dogs would have a field day. Everyone scrambled out of the station wagon and chased rabbits in our good Sunday clothes. We ended up being late for church that Sunday (a definite sin in Dad's book).

Some of our neighboring farm families had horses. We begged Dad for a horse. We never got the horse we wanted, but Dad did buy us a tired old pony to ride. I was afraid of the pony because he bit. And he bit hard. But the boys didn't care; they loved that pony. They took turns riding bareback; we didn't have a saddle. The pony got lots of exercise.

One summer day, David decided to ride the pony to the end of the lane and get the mail for Mom. He led the pony out of the barn and put the bridle on, all by himself. That was a job for a guy no taller then the pony. He guided the pony over to the step at the barn door, and mounted. He proudly rode down the lane to the mailbox all by himself. When he got to the mailbox he discovered he could not maneuver the pony close enough to get the mail. He had to get off to reach the mailbox. Now he had a dilemma. How to get back on the pony? There were no steps at the end of the lane. There was just a quiet country road and a mailbox. He realized he had to walk the pony back up the lane.

Since he didn't want to be seen by his brothers because they would torment him about his inability to get back on the pony, he decided to run back up the lane as quickly as he could. He did not want to be seen leading the pony instead of riding him. The problem however was how fast could he run? His best running speed was somewhere between a trot and a gallop for the pony. So the pony did the only thing he could do, he galloped. When David realized the pony was gaining on him and would soon run him over he tried to increase his speed. But his little legs could not go any faster. Down he went as the pony galloped right over him. Mail went flying everywhere, as David let go of the reins and the mail. David lifted his head and looked up the lane from his vantage point on the ground. There he saw his older brother Dan, at the top of the lane watching the whole incident. Dan was laughing so hard he nearly wet himself. But he did recover well enough to catch the runaway pony. Dave never rode alone again.

During the time we had the pony, our cousin Tony from the city was staying with us. My Aunt Lorie felt a summer on the farm would be good for Tony. He was a good helper to Dad even if a little ignorant about the country. And he loved that pony. Being a skinny, gangly teenager he was not too heavy for the pony. However, his legs were a little long. With no saddle with stirrups, his legs dangled down either side of the pony and would drag along the ground as he rode. He just let them drag as he happily took his rides through the fields.

In the evening when the chores were done, Tony and the boys went out and played Cowboys and Indians until after dark. The sight of Tony on that pony with all the boys lined up on either side of him as they came over the hill at sunset put me to mind of a scene in a TV western. First a head appeared. Then a couple more with toy guns in their hands pointed at the sky. The pony would come into view with Tony mounted like the chief. All he was missing was the war bonnet. With the sun setting in the West, I half expected to see credits role.

If anyone got too close, the pony bit an arm or back. And he bit hard. I definitely didn't get too close if he didn't want me there. But taking care of a pony was a good experience for the boys. Other chores they did around the farm were supervised and checked by Dad but the pony was totally their responsibility.

Spending the evening together away from the hospital is relaxing. We are enjoying each other's company, even though we can see how tired everyone is. We have fun looking at Mom's wall of fame. There are so many kids, grandkids and even a great granddaughter; Mom finds it difficult to display pictures of everyone in her house. Dad helped her solve the problem by covering one wall of the family room with corkboard. Mom hung all of our graduation pictures. They are lined up according to age at the top of the corkboard. Under each graduation picture is a picture of each of our husbands or wives, below that the grandchildren and below that the one great grandchild. She shows everyone visiting the house her wall of photos. Pointing out each child, their mate and children and telling them all about us. Tears came to my eyes as I imagined her showing off her family.

We are a long way from home in Ohio. But we feel at home in Mom's house. We've seen an improvement in Mom. I know we need to think about going home. Again, there are mixed emotions. No one wants to leave Mom but everyone has responsibilities back home. We will have to get back to Ohio soon.

# Chapter Ten

## *Keeping Them Straight*

Visiting Mom the next day is less stressful. We know she will recover so everyone is relaxed. Sue and Jane are the first to see her in the morning. We are surprised when, no sooner had they left the waiting room than they are back giggling, like teenagers. Between fits of laughter they explain. When they entered Mom's room, they immediately backed out before she saw them. Mom is sitting up in bed with her eyes closed. When she is not feeling well, she has a habit of running her fingers through her hair. She must have been doing it this morning, because her hair is standing straight out all over her head. Adding the effect of her large glasses, which magnify her eyes, and the absence of dentures, she looks just like a little troll doll sitting in the bed. If she could see herself she would have quite a laugh. It takes Sue and Jane several minutes to get themselves under control so they can go into Mom's room without laughing. It is a good thing the rest of us are forewarned; when we take our turn visiting her we're prepared. It is good to be able to be more relaxed around Mom. Thank God the crisis is over.

When it is finally my turn to see Mom, a nurse is checking her IV and asks how she ever kept track of so many kids. Tired from her morning round of visitors and answering so many questions about raising her kids, Mom snapped, "You just do."

How they kept track of all those kids is a question I sometimes ask myself. I am sure it wasn't easy. Several times kids were left behind or forgotten in the crowd. And with so many of us, we were often called by another's name.

As if one name per kid wasn't enough, Dad loved to give nicknames. Everyone had at least one nickname. Mine was an embarrassment to me, especially when I was a teenager. It was, 'Doe doe'. That was all I could say when I was 2. Dad said I walked around the house all day saying, 'Doe doe'. Dad nicknamed David 'Pete'. Rose was 'Rosebud' and Sue was 'Sueboo'. Marie was shortened to 'Mitt' and Gerard was 'Willie' and sometimes 'Beetle Bailey' when he did something that reminded Dad of a fresh recruit in the Army. Grandma Foltz was unhappy with Dad's use of nicknames for the kids and never hesitated to tell him so. The name "Willie" was the one she hated the most. She told Dad he should have named him William if he was going to call him Willie.

Jerry had one of the worst nicknames, 'Pooper'. He earned the name. When there was work to be done Jerry would often announce he had to go to the bathroom. Off he would go, but seldom returned before the work was just about done. Dad never seemed to notice he was gone and he got out of a lot of work that way.

The younger kids got their nicknames from the older ones. Vince was 'Hypo' for his temper tantrums, and Bernie was 'Bird Turd'. For some reason Tim got 'Hubbard'. When Andy was learning to read he would sound out anything he could find with printing on it. Bernie caught him trying to read the side of an apple basket from the Hanson Apple Orchard. He teased him and called him 'Hanson' and it stuck. New friends couldn't keep up with who was who.

Grandma Foltz hated all the nicknames, not just 'Willie'. She would shake her finger at Dad and say; "Roy, you gave good Christian names to these children; use them." Dad would just shake his head and walk away. Grandma had 16 kids of her own and called each one by their given name. Like many mothers-in-law, Grandma didn't think Dad was quite good enough for her daughter Alice.

When Mom had a new baby Grandma often came to stay, watch us and help Mom get settled with the new little one. The entire time Mom was in the hospital, sometimes several days, Grandma would lecture Dad every minute she could about what he should do for Mom. Her list was endless. Build this, expand that and repair this. She would say, "You're a carpenter. Why don't you do these things?" Dad would sit there silently, steam seemed to be rolling from his ears, rush through his dinner and head for the barn for some peace and quiet. He never talked back to her, just nodded and got away as fast as he could.

It's not like Dad never did anything to the houses we lived in. He was endlessly remodeling or fixing up some part of the house. Mom always had beautiful kitchens with oak cabinets and modern appliances. She had nice countertops, and Dad kept the floors new. Cabinet making and kitchen remodeling were in his line of work and it was something he could do for Mom. She loved it. He would use the newest laminates for counter tops. And Mom's cabinets always had the latest features like drawers that glided in and out with little effort. He was rewarded with lots of homemade treats from the kitchens he designed for Mom.

One chore Dad hated was painting. Mom didn't mind painting, so she did it. When she felt the rooms needed brightening she bought cheap pastel paint and did the work herself. It always seemed to give her a lift to put a fresh coat of paint on the walls. And we enjoyed the refreshing color change in our bedrooms. This was about the extent of redecorating when I was a kid. Sometimes we got new plastic curtains for the bedroom windows at the farm. There wasn't money for expensive drapes or blinds.

Having your own bedroom was rare. I had my own room when the family was smaller, but as more kids came, bedrooms got crowded. Dad built bunk beds to stack the boys. We had a four bedroom house, so most of the time we were crowded. Some bedrooms had two sets of bunk beds so four kids could use the room. That worked best for the boys since there were so many of them. In Louisville, when there were 13 kids in the house, we had three huge walk-in closets. They were about 15 feet long by six feet wide. All three closets had a little window at one end. I begged Dad to let me use one for a bedroom. My bed, a desk and a dresser would fit in the closet easily. Mom was concerned that people would think she was reduced to storing kids in closets and didn't want me in there. I finally convinced them I needed the privacy and they gave me one of the closets. I had my best friend come over and help me paint the walls with cheap blue water-based paint. It was great. We had a ball painting it, and I had some privacy.

Storage space such as dressers was always in short supply. We each usually had two drawers and shared closet space. Mom insisted we put our clean clothes away in the drawers. She did not want clothes piled around the room. Having enough dressers was important to her. Things needed to be in their place and that included everybody's clothes. Mom used to tell me the dresser story from when Nancy and I were little. I never tired of hearing it.

When David was born Mom had four little ones. One day Dad came home to find Mom crying. She had a case of the new mother blues. Taking care of four little ones, including Nancy with her health problems had her feeling down. When Dad asked her what was wrong she cried and said she didn't even have enough dresser space to store the children's clothes. He sat her down and soothed her jangled nerves and had her laughing in no time. The next day he came home from work with a little unfinished oak dresser. He carefully sanded and stained the 36-inch tall dresser. It didn't even need hardware for the drawers. Two handle spaces were notched in the wood on each of the four little drawer fronts. Mom loved her new dresser, and carefully stored the baby clothes for each new child in the little dresser.

Over the years the little dresser took plenty of abuse. The top was stained and the varnish peeled from all the bottles that were placed on it over the years. Steam from the vaporizer she used all night whenever a little one had a cold, caused the wood to swell, making the drawers hard to open sometimes. That caused strain on the drawers and eventually they began to come apart. Stuffing too many clothes in each drawer loosened the joint, too. After nearly 15 years of use for each new baby, the little dresser was falling apart. Mom still loved it, but Dad didn't think it was worth fixing and wanted to throw it away. When I was expecting my first child, Mom offered it to me for my baby's clothes. She said she didn't want to throw it away and maybe my husband could fix it up for my new baby. I was delighted.

I took the dresser and my husband repaired it. He sanded it down and applied a fresh coat of varnish. I've kept the dresser and hope to hand it down through the family someday.

Even with plenty of closet and dresser space, keeping your room clean was impossible with so many others sharing the space. It was an ongoing struggle to get everyone to make their bed and pick up after themselves. Thursday was upstairs cleaning day. In the summer we all helped with our rooms. During the school year everyone stripped their beds and took the bedding to the laundry room every Thursday morning. When we got home from school the clean bedding was waiting for us to put back on the beds. Sheets were in short supply. With so many beds, having more than a sheet for each bed would have been a luxury. We only had one sheet to cover the mattress. A top sheet was a luxury reserved for guests. If we had a friend stay the night we got two sheets.

When I was small Mom hung the laundry outside in the summer and in the basement in the winter. She called the basement a cellar, and some of us still do today. When I was a teenager we purchased our first electric dryer, but Mom only used it when she had to. She hung the clothes outside whenever possible, for the fresh scent and to save money.

We wondered over the years how Mom managed to get the correct underwear, socks, and pajamas to the right kids. In the mornings, the piles of laundry were a gigantic hodgepodge of color and fabric, but by afternoon it seemed to magically turn into neat, organized stacks of fresh clean clothes. Each child took their own stack of clothes to their room and stored them away in their dresser drawers. Laundry was not a weekly happening. The more kids Mom had the more often she did laundry. For a while it was a daily chore.

When we needed more bedroom space Dad added a bedroom in the basement for the older boys. They loved it. There was an exterior door in the basement and they could sneak out after dark to play or go to the neighbors without Mom and Dad knowing. The boys were not very neat about their rooms. I preferred to stay out of their rooms between cleanings. I never knew what I'd find there.

Beside kids and clothes to keep track of there were other things Moms have to do every day for their kids. Homework, for instance. She had to make sure everyone had his or her homework done each night. Most of the girls were good about homework but some of the boys hated it, and went to great lengths to avoid sitting around the kitchen table doing boring homework. The boys were adventurers, not scholars. Mom had a major job on her hands keeping nine boys caught up on homework. Since the boys had chores to do after school, homework was an after-supper job. There was a circle of kids, heads bent over books and papers, some with feet swinging just short of reaching the floor sitting around the kitchen table every school night. Mom would often be feeding graham crackers soaked in warm milk to newest baby (hoping he would sleep through the night) as she supervised the reluctant study group. Occasional wails of 'I can't do this' would result in help from Mom or an older sibling.

Getting our finished homework to school the next day was our job. With that many kids going out the door each morning, Mom couldn't make sure we had everything we needed. In the morning we gathered our books and homework, grabbed a packed lunch off the counter and got ourselves out the door on time. We were the ones to suffer the consequences of forgotten books, homework or lunch. The fear of the nuns was an excellent incentive to remember your homework. That's a good way to teach responsibility.

With so many to keep track of, it was inevitable that at some point a kid would be left behind by accident. When we were all loaded into the station wagon to go home from some adventure, Mom would shout from the front seat, "Is everybody here?" Well, since we were there, we would yell, "Yeah", and off we'd go, only to get down the road and discover someone was missing. It was frightening to be the one missing once you realized the rest of the family was gone.

After one hot summer day at the local pool, Mom gathered up her kids and loaded up the blankets, towels, and beach toys and headed to the car. After loading everything and getting the kids into the car she slid behind the wheel. Before starting the car she asked, "Is everybody here?" "Yeah" was the reply from the group. As she drove out the exit, and down the road past the pool toward home, a lifeguard came running across the grass, waving his arms to get Mom's attention; a sobbing Jane, long wet hair flowing behind her, stumbling along after him.

The worst such incident, however, was on a family trip to Florida. After stopping at a rest stop the inevitable question was heard from the front of the pickup truck, "is everybody here?" Then the standard answer, "Yeah" was shouted in unison from the back. The family was off, refreshed and ready to resume the trip. A few miles down the highway someone asked, "Where's Vince?" Checking around, they realized he was nowhere to be found. Oh, No!! A missing kid!! On the freeway to Florida! Mom was frantic. Dad made an illegal U turn immediately and beat it back to the rest stop. There was Vince, looking small and forlorn, sitting on the curb where the pickup truck had been parked, crying, convinced he was forever lost. He was more careful from then on and made it back to the truck before everyone else.

Keeping track of kids was just about as hard as keeping them straight. Hand me down clothes were a way of life and Mom would often identify kids by the clothes they were wearing. If the outfit had just been handed down from one kid to another there was confusion as to who was standing there.

One evening at dinner Gerard had done something to irritate Dad at the table. Dad turned to Gerard and said "What did I tell you, Jerry, ah Dave, ah Bernie, ah Dan, ah, whatever your name is?"

To Dad's surprise, Gerard burst into tears. Dad asked, "Now what are you crying about?" To which Gerard replied through a shower of tears, "You don't even know my name." I can understand his feeling of being lost in the crowd.

We became accustomed to being called each other's names, but what we really hated was being called by our full name. That meant we were in big trouble. Many times our full name was followed by the command, "Go out and get a switch off a tree. And make it a big one!" Remarkably, we would actually get the switch and return for our punishment. Then someone realized that if we just disappeared instead of bringing a switch back, and didn't return until the next meal, Mom would forgot the offense and we were off the hook. Life was a little sweeter after that.

My brothers had a knack for disappearing for hours. They went to the far reaches of the farm and invented all kinds of games. Before they left the house they would sneak food from the kitchen or raid the garden. They even went so far as to sneak whole chickens from the freezer to roast them over a campfire pretending to be campers, Indians or soldiers. They drank water from wherever they found it, in creeks, or in the water trough the cows used. Whether the water was drinkable or not didn't cross anyone's mind. Water was clean and fresh on the farm. Mom was happy to have them out of her hair and knew that they wouldn't leave the area they were permitted to play in. They played for hours down by the creek, often getting soaked in the process. If there was water around they were in it.

All the kids loved to go places with Dad. They would hide in the back of the pickup truck under a tarp whenever they knew he had to go into town for something. Whoever was hiding waited until he got too far down the road to take the time to go back. Then they popped up in the back window and waved at him. He'd just shake his head and keep driving. They thought they were pulling a fast one, but Dad knew they were back there. He loved the company on his errands.

When Nancy and I were small, Dad drove a school bus for extra money. He did his morning route and parked the bus at the house for the day. In the afternoon he took the kids home from school and returned the bus to the school district garage for the night. We were not permitted to play in or around the school bus. It was off limits to little kids. Sometimes in the afternoon we would sneak onto the bus and hide under the seats so we could ride along with Dad on the route. We were too young to go to school and being on the bus with big kids was a thrill. Besides, our Dad was the bus driver. To us that made him like a king and we were his kids. After getting away with our little prank a few times Dad started checking under all the seats for little kids before leaving for his afternoon run. As a treat he allowed us to go with him sometimes. Only one at a time and we were permitted to sit on the heater right by Dad. What fun!

As I lean on the window ledge in Mom's room and watch her talk to the nurse, sadness comes over me. Tomorrow I will be leaving Florida. Leaving my mother to the care of others. I will not be here to make sure she has good care. I will not be able to touch her, see her smile and watch her improve. I won't really know she is getting better. Leaving is not going to be easy. But I know she has great faith in God. Faith that whatever the future brings, she will be able to handle it as she has all these years. I need to put my faith in Him, too. The only part I can play in her recovery is prayer. I will be praying for her every day I'm away from her.

# Chapter 11

## *Holidays*

As I stand here feeling a little blue, an attendant arrives with Mom's lunch tray. As she sweeps into the room and deposits the tray on the bedside table she asks if this was the lady with all the kids she's been hearing so much about. Her mood improved, Mom says; "Yep, that's me." As the attendant takes the cover off Mom's entree she has just one question. "What were the holidays like at your house?" That brought a smile to Mom's face, and I have to laugh just thinking about holidays. What fun we had.

Christmas is for kids, and in our house there were a lot of them. Mom was always excited about Christmas. So much so that she often couldn't wait until Christmas morning. Some years Santa would arrive early at our house. I remember a year Dad took all of us to Christmas Eve services at our church, St. Mary's in Morges. Only the baby at the time, Bernie, stayed home with Mom.

As children spilled from the car, I breathed in the crisp winter air, and noticed the stars, so plentiful in the clear sky. As I walked toward the house, wrapping my coat tightly around me, I looked up into the dark sky. I was sure there had never been more stars in the sky or a more perfect Christmas Eve. The beautiful night was made better by the excitement of the little ones, anticipating Santa's arrival by morning. The older kids reveled in the excitement generated by the innocent believers. I could see the Christmas tree we had decorated as it lit the window in the living room. The little kids skipped around me heading toward the warmth of the house.

What a surprise awaited them. When we stepped into the living room we found that Santa had already been there, while we were at church. The room was overflowing with toys and gifts. Not just under the tree. The whole room was filled with toys. Mom didn't spend money on wrapping paper, so everything was in sight. It was like a child's dream, all the gleaming toy trucks and cars for the boys. There were toy tractors and wagons, boxes of army men and bags of shiny new marbles. New dolls and sets of toy dishes with little pots and pans for the little girls, games in shiny new boxes, books and new outfits for everyone. Squeals of delight and shouts of joy accompanied a stampede into the room. Mom was nearly knocked over as the boys and girls ran past her to check out the treasures.

After we explored all the new toys and gifts, someone thought to question Mom about Santa. After all, she had actually been in the house and awake when he came. "Just think," a little one said. "If we hadn't been at church, we would have been here, too." The kids could have seen Santa.

With a most serious expression, Mom explained she had been upstairs putting the baby to bed and missed the whole thing. She thought she heard something downstairs but assumed we had returned from church early. So she didn't investigate the noise. When the baby was asleep, she returned to the living room, and found it filled with toys. Sadly, Santa was gone. She looked out the window, but there was no sign of him anywhere. She told a pretty convincing story. The older kids enjoyed the secret as much as Mom and Dad did.

Funny thing, the kids never thought to ask Mom how she knew what gifts were for which kid. Most years the Christmas gifts weren't wrapped and had no tag on them. There were a few years though, when all the gifts were wrapped. Mom somehow got a huge roll of Halli's Department Store wrapping paper. It was white paper with Halli's written in fancy gold script. The store, in Cleveland, did gift-wrapping for customers. How she got the paper I never knew. All the gifts were wrapped in that same paper for three years in a row. Whenever we talk about Christmas someone in the group always says "remember that Halli's paper!' which is always followed by laughter. No one will ever forget that paper.

As the kids grew up and learned who Santa really was, their curiosity always got the better of them. It became a contest each year to see who could find the loot before Christmas. Once someone located one of Mom's hiding places and discovered gifts, they could not keep their secret and shared their find with their closest pal in the family. They would swear the lucky conspirator to secrecy and take them to see the discovery. Then, the new conspirator showed someone else and so it went until all the non-believers had seen the loot.

The boys were the worst for searching out the hiding places. Mom realized what was going on and was constantly on the lookout for new hiding places. One year Dad really fooled the boys. He waited until Christmas Eve Day to go to a local store to shop for the boys. They all got new Tonka trucks. Those wonderful sturdy metal trucks, painted yellow with working toy construction equipment to match. For once they had no idea what would be under the tree.

Another year Dad thought he found a great hiding place. He had a small boat the family used in the summer at Atwood Lake. It was stored for the winter in a shed on the property where Dad had his cabinet shop. He took the Christmas gifts and put them in the boat. Surely no one would think to look in a boat stored away for the winter. But the boys left no stone unturned in the annual search for toys. They not only discovered the hiding place, they played with the toys in the shed for hours, then carefully packed them back in the boxes, just as they had found them. The most fun toy in the shed was a set of guns that shot Nerf® balls. The balls were soft foam and could be used indoors without damaging anything. There were three balls for each gun. The boys had a blast in that shed, having shootouts and target practice. They played so intently in the crowded storage shed that some of the balls got lost among all the stored items. There was lumber, old tools, lawn and garden equipment, old paint cans and even a few tires. It was impossible to find all the missing Nerf® balls. After an exhaustive search the boys had to give up. They packed the guns away without the balls. That's how Mom and Dad found out hiding Christmas presents in the boat wouldn't work either.

When the kids found hidden Christmas gifts, no one knew what gift was for which kid. There were times when someone got excited about the prospect of many happy hours of play with one of the Christmas treasures they found, only to be disappointed on Christmas morning when the gift went to someone else. However, being taught to share meant a toy not destined to belong to you was still available for your enjoyment.

Every kid remembers a favorite Christmas. Like Gerard. His favorite Christmas was when he got his beloved red wagon. That morning when the kids ran down the stairs there were shiny new bikes (some not so new, but who cared) lined up in a row for Dan, David and Rose. On the other side of the room there were two bright new tricycles for Marie and Sue. And right in the middle of the room was the shiny new red Radio Flyer wagon of his dreams. He spent most of Christmas Day just sitting in his treasured wagon, in the middle of the living room hardly believing it was really his.

Dan and David remember the year they got BB guns. They were 8 and 6 years old, and Dad insisted that boys needed to learn to hunt, so they got their first guns. Mom was upset. She was sure that, as the saying went in those days "they'll shoot their eye out." She was so frantic and upset at Dad; she felt the boys were just too young. At least if he was giving them guns he could remove the pins so they would not really fire. So Dad took out the firing pins. Dan and Dave didn't care. They had guns. Just like Dad when he went hunting. I can picture the two of them, trudging through a snow covered field, all bundled up in heavy winter coats and stocking hats, carrying their guns, safely pointed at the ground as Dad had taught them, on their way to hunt like men. But as David says now, "the only way we were going to get any rabbits with those guns would be to club 'em to death."

New sleds were wonderful Christmas gifts. They were usually a group gift. Like the new sled Dan and David got one year. It had bright red metal runners, and beautifully varnished boards with the brand name printed in big red letters down the centerboard. It looked like a million bucks, new and shiny standing against the wall beside the tree. They couldn't wait to try it out.

We had a wonderful sledding hill above the barn. It was very steep and about 200 feet long. The hill was so steep it provided the fast and furious ride the boys loved. There was a fence at the bottom of the hill with an opening wide enough for the tractor and hay wagon. From the opening in the fence it was a straight shot to the wide double barn doors.

After chores were done, Dan proudly pulled the new sled to the top of the hill, straight above the fence opening. David trailed along behind him. As they trudged up the hill, warmly bundled against the cold, Dan told David he would teach him how to control the sled before David took his first run down the hill. David had never used a sled like this and he had no idea how to steer it. Hopping up and down with excitement, David didn't want to wait for a long lesson from his older brother.

Dan positioned the sled at the top of the hill, facing downward and turned around to explain the fine art of sledding to his little brother. Not wanting to wait for his ride, David dropped onto the sled on his stomach and went sailing down the hill. Not knowing how to control it, he was at the mercy of gravity. As he sailed down the hill toward the barn, laughing out loud, he soon realized he didn't know how to turn the sled. He lay on his stomach on the shiny new sled and just held onto the wooden handles, not realizing that pushing forward on each side would steer him right or left. When he raised his head and looked up, he saw a barn window fast approaching. He closed his eyes, put his

100

head down, and braced himself for the impact. As he careened toward the barn he wished he had listened to his brother. At an incredible rate of speed he crashed right through the window, landing on the back of a very startled cow and fell, sled and all, in the unpleasant debris of the barn floor. Dan had been running behind him as fast as he could. He found David and the sled covered with cow manure. Thankfully David, the cow, and the sled were all unharmed.

But, there was a broken window to contend with. One of the things Dad really hated was a broken window. When David had to face Dad he wished he had listened to Dan and learned how to control the sled first.

The girls had less dangerous toys. Sue for example, fondly remembers her 'Easy Bake Oven'. Like most of the girls, she wanted to be just like Mom in the kitchen. Whenever Mom baked a cake or cookies, she gave some batter to Sue to bake in her little oven. It amazed her that a simple light bulb could bake a miniature cake or cookie. Sue shared her creations with other kids, but in that crowd it didn't go far. Ever the little hostess, she carefully cut the little cake in as many as six pieces and proudly served it to her guests.

Rose's favorite Christmas gift was a tape recorder. She still has it. She had a lot of fun with that machine. It was a simple flat recorder popular in the late '60s. The sound quality wasn't good but that didn't matter. She remembers enjoying helping Mom prove a point to Dad. He snored. Like many people who snore, he denied it. He refused to believe Mom when she complained about his loud snoring. One evening after a big dinner, satisfied and content, Dad fell asleep in his favorite chair, as he often did. Relaxed, he started snoring. Mom told Rose to quietly get her tape recorder. Whispering conspiratorially, they taped him snoring, then waited till he woke up to happily play the tape back to him. A red-faced Dad had to admit he snored as he got up from the chair, grumbling under his breath, and went outside to escape the peals of laughter. Mom and Rose were about rolling on the floor.

All the kids got into the spirit of giving. Mostly they wanted to give something to Mom for Christmas. They never had much money of their own. So, Dad took them shopping and matched whatever money they had saved for gift giving. They climbed into the car for the drive uptown to the five and dime store. They walked around and around the displays trying to find just the right gift for a special Mom. When she opened their gift, they wanted her to just about jump out of her seat with excitement. That's a lot to ask from a gift worth a dollar or two. Kitchen gadgets were a frequent gift. Considering the time she spent in the kitchen, it seemed like a good choice to little kids. She often received knives, measuring cups, dishcloths and dishtowels. No matter what she opened on Christmas, Mom acted like it was one of the best gifts she'd ever received.

As the kids got older and earned their own money they enjoyed buying gifts for their younger brothers and sisters. I remember buying all the little boys remote control cars. It was so much fun watching them open the cars, insert batteries and run a half a dozen cars all over the room. Everywhere you looked a remote control car was crashing into furniture, running under tables, or into someone's feet. It was total chaos, but it was the best kind of chaos.

Dan and David once pooled their money to buy cork guns for their younger brothers. The younger boys were so excited. But Dan and David bought themselves even bigger ones. They had to be able to outshoot the little guys.

Oh, and the Christmas trees we decorated! It was always a fresh cut tree. The tree stand was a yearly struggle for Dad. They never invented one that worked. The tree trunk was seldom straight. Most of the time the tree wouldn't stand up at all, let alone straight. Dad used a variety of makeshift methods to get the tree to stay upright in the stand, including fastening it to the wall on more than one occasion. It took a great deal of time to get it straight and find a side of the tree without a hole that you could turn to the front. When Dad picked out the tree, it looked great on the lot.

Once he got it in the house, it was a different story. We learned to stay out of the way until the tree was secured.

Dad was in charge of attaching the lights. We had those wonderful huge bulbs that burnt hot. We were always afraid of a tree fire, after Dad's annual lecture on the dangers of leaving the lights on too long. After the tree was secured and the lights attached, the kids took over and Dad disappeared. It was always a beautiful tree, no matter how bad it looked. Most of the ornaments were placed near the bottom, where little kids could reach the branches. As the kids grew taller, the ornaments were hung higher. Strings of popcorn and colorful chains made of construction paper added to the tree's charm. The grand finale of tree trimming was the application of icicles. These sparkling silver strands were saved from year to year. Throwing them away was wasteful. Mom preferred not to buy new ones every year. She would patiently show us how to place them carefully on the branches, one at a time; but the kids would lose patience and throw handfuls of knotted and jumbled icicles all over the tree and the surrounding area.

But when we were finished, Mom and Dad didn't change a thing on the tree. It was a tree for kids decorated by kids. They declared it the best looking tree ever, as we gathered around, very proud of it.

Christmas day was spent at the 'hall'. After church we piled into the car to attend the annual gathering of Mom's family. My mother's family was so large (she had 15 brothers and sisters) that each Christmas a hall was rented for Christmas Day so they and their children could be together for the holiday. Everyone brought covered dishes for dinner and spent the day together. We enjoyed the day with all of our favorite cousins. The adults spent time catching up with the latest gossip, playing euchre for hours and eating until they were stuffed. The kids ran through the hall, in and out the doors and generally exhausted themselves. New games, just opened that morning, kept kids occupied. Christmas is about family and we were part of a large and loving one.

Easter was spent with Mom's family at a hall, too. But the best part of Easter was the candy. There was never a lot of candy, but each kid got the traditional chocolate bunny, marshmallow peeps and jelly beans. And we colored eggs. Mom cooked 10 dozen eggs. We loved to dye them pink, blue, yellow, green and violet. What a mess we made as we spent Saturday afternoon gathered around the table dipping boiled eggs in cups of dye. Each of us wanted to make the prettiest egg. A variety of combinations were tried, and some of the results were pretty bad. Dad was the master of egg coloring. He bought fancy coloring kits with oil paint and made some really different eggs. But it didn't matter what they looked like; each kid thought his was the best and Mom never disagreed.

Finding your basket on the kitchen table in the morning and exploring the contents was almost as exciting as Christmas. However, if we were old enough to go to Communion at Easter Sunday Mass we couldn't eat any of the candy until we got home from church. Most of us gave up candy for lent and we couldn't wait for that first sweet taste of the forbidden treats.

We bartered on Easter Sunday morning. If we didn't like something in our basket we could trade with someone else. Trades were discussed at length; counteroffers made, and deals struck for flavors of jellybeans, marshmallow peeps, and foil-covered eggs.

Going to church on Easter Sunday was special. Everyone dressed in his or her new Easter clothes and even if it was cold, there was the excitement of spring in the air. We each had a new Sunday outfit, including new dress shoes. It felt so good to get all dressed up for church on Easter Sunday. The girls wore frilly dresses with white socks and white or black patent leather shoes. When I was small there were new spring coats and little white gloves. But the crowning touch was the Easter bonnet. Hats were required for girls in church and new Easter hats made us feel so special, as Mom placed them on our heads and sang "In your Easter Bonnet."

The boys had new dress pants, shirts and ties. Each boy had shiny new shoes with no scuff marks. They were told to stay clean until we were ready to leave for church. They didn't always succeed. On at least one Sunday, Mom wanted to see the boys in spotless outfits. In spite of Mom's efforts to wet down their hair and combed it just so the cowlicks would spring right back up. The new outfits were our Sunday attire for the summer. On Easter Sunday morning we felt like a million bucks walking into the church. Mom checked us over before leaving for church and declared us perfect Easter Sunday children.

Halloween was another annual treat for the kids. Mom was not enthused about this holiday. She never had the money for fancy costumes. She wasn't creative, so making our costumes wasn't easy for her. We were usually ghosts. That one was easy. An old sheet and a scissors were all Mom needed to create a band of ghosts. Or you could be a hobo. There were plenty of old clothes around, making it easy to dress up like a bum. Smear dirt on our faces and the costume was complete. Mom sent us out in any old costume she could find. But we loved it. The fun wasn't the costume; it was being set free, after dark, too see how many treats we could get in two hours. When we lived on the farm there weren't many houses to visit in the neighborhood, so Mom took us to Grandma's in town. Grandma had lots of neighbors in the city.

When we got home from our trick-or-treat adventures, the candy was put in a large bowl. We kept our favorite treat, but Mom knew that unsupervised, we would make ourselves sick eating too much at one time. Each day we had a treat from the bowl. Mom and Dad enjoyed the candy as much as we did and it was a lesson in sharing.

Those lessons have served us well. Right now we are sharing our love and concern for Mom. With so many shoulders to lean on we can get through anything together. As Mom eats her lunch I lean on the windowsill watching her. I know I gave her a hard time sometimes as I grew up.

105

We weren't good at expressing the things we felt deeply. I want to tell her how much I love her and appreciate all she did for me, but I can't without breaking down. Right now she looks so relaxed I don't want to upset her with my tears. Besides, Mom has always been a no nonsense person. She never seemed comfortable showing her feelings. Maybe later, when others are not around, we can talk.

# Chapter Twelve

## *Vacations*

There are people in and out of Mom's room continuously. They take good care of her and I am grateful. As nurses check her vital signs, adjust her IV's and dispense medication they are talkative and friendly. We enjoy answering some of the questions they ask. Another question we answer concerns vacations; did we take vacation trips? How could my parents ever afford to take vacations with such a large family? The answer for many years is they didn't.

When I was small we never went on a vacation. We traveled to Florida in the winter for Nancy's health, but those trips weren't vacations. We lived in Florida in the winter, and Dad got a job. The beaches were fun on the weekends. But we weren't in Florida to vacation.

Sometimes we needed a break from each other. Mom seemed to know when each of us needed time away from the rest. She sent us to stay with a relative or friend for a few days. These mini vacations meant a lot to us. It gave us a chance to feel special and get some breathing room. Being an individual in such a large family is difficult. We sometimes felt lost in the crowd. When Mom sensed this, she gave us a vacation away from the other kids. I remember going to stay with Mom's friend Peg and her family. She had daughters my age and they lived a different lifestyle then I did. I marveled at all they had: their own room, toys they did not share, no brothers to drive them crazy. Their house seemed so quiet compared to ours. They lived in the city, and I was amazed the first time I saw a 'bookmobile' come to the neighborhood. They could borrow books, and two weeks later the bookmobile came back so they could return them and borrow other books. We didn't have bookmobiles in the country and the only place I could borrow books was the school library.

We came home from our little getaways refreshed. As I look back I wonder at Mom's wisdom and her ability to know just what we needed.

When we lived on the farm, family vacations were out of the question. There wasn't money or time to travel. Besides, Dad worked a regular construction job so weekends and any free time he could get was spent working on the farm.

After years of struggling to make a living as a farmer, Dad finally gave it up and sold the farm. It was hard for him to do. He loved life in the country and thought it was the best place to raise a family. Leaving it wasn't something he chose easily. But he was always working and missing out on the joys of life. With a regular job, milking cows every morning and evening, working all weekend planting, harvesting and maintaining the place there was no time left for the family.

He expected the boys to work like adults, which deprived them of the fun of just being kids. He was stressed out, trying to make a go of the farm and support such a large family. Under such stress his temper was getting the best of him and things weren't always pleasant around the house. It was time to give up the farm and move on.

Dad and Mom bought a place with a couple of acres in Dad's hometown of Louisville, Ohio. There was space for a big garden and a few animals. He knew many people in the area and was soon content to work at his craft of carpentry and cabinet making. After working for a contractor, Dad purchased his own cabinet shop and made a business for himself. He said it was the best financial move he ever made. Life was easier, the money was not so tight, and things changed for the better in our crowded home.

Now there was time for vacations, but not much money to spend on such luxuries. A very dear friend of Dad's, Dave Hoobler enjoyed camping with his family. We visited them at their campsite at Leesville Lake one hot summer Sunday. Mom and Dad enjoyed the day, the idea of camping with the family was born. It was inexpensive and they could take the kids on a budget. The great outdoors, with lots of room for the kids to play and have wonderful adventures, appealed to everyone. To find out if they would like camping, they bought a large tent and a few pieces of equipment. They loaded the kids in the car and off they went to Atwood Lake for the weekend. A campsite was minimal in cost and the kids could spend time swimming, hiking and just hanging out. Soon the kids were taking their bikes, and soaking up the fresh air and sunshine. They liked the freedom they had in the park. They met lots of kids their age. The kids helped pack what they needed for the trips and enthusiastically loaded the car for each outing. It was a perfect setup for this large and energetic bunch.

Camping was not much of a vacation for Mom. She cooked and baked for days before the family left. She had to pack the food and make sure everyone had everything they needed. Then unpack everything on Sunday evening when they arrived back home. There were mountains of laundry to do on Mondays. But Mom loved it. They often camped with some of Mom's brothers and their families. They met and made friends with other camping enthusiasts. Hours of relaxing at the campsite enjoying friends and family, with less kids underfoot, was a break for her. This became the preferred summer activity. The family went camping every weekend if possible. Mom sometimes went to the lake earlier in the week and Dad joined them after work, going back to work the next day.

The kids let loose when they were camping. They snuck out after dark to meet friends and walk around the park and talk for hours. Then they'd sneak back in and Mom never knew they had been gone. They could choose activities they truly enjoyed and spend hours at the beach or on the trails.

After the family discovered how much they all loved camping, Mom and Dad invested in a small camper. Mom and the kids found it a lot easier to pack the camper than the car. The boys slept in the tent, but the girls slept in the camper with Mom, Dad and the baby. As kids got older and had job responsibilities they couldn't always go with the family. But they all have fond memories of camping.

Since the family loved the water and camped at a lake, Dad decided to buy a boat. It was just a small one but they loved it. There was always a bunch of kids climbing all over that boat. Dad piled them all in and took them to the beach area for the day. Dad got a campsite on the water so the boat was right there to enjoy.

Since camping was the best vacation idea for the family, Mom and Dad bought a lot at Springwood Campground about 25 miles from home. With a lot they could keep the camper there year round, instead of loading and unloading all the time. The place had a nice pool, and a pond, with plans for a lake. The kids loved the tennis courts and playground. There were family activities planned all summer long. Clearing the lot at Springwood was a family project. Everyone helped clear brush, cut down trees and gather rocks. The entire family worked to make it a home away from home. The guard at the entrance gate came to expect the regular Friday night arrival of the station wagon full of kids.

A trip to Florida was the first real vacation for the family. Dan, Dave, Rose and I were older and didn't go with them. So 10 kids rode in the pickup truck with a cap over the bed. Behind the truck, they pulled the small camper trailer. The two smallest kids rode in the cab with Mom and Dad, and eight kids took the trip in the bed of the truck. They went in the winter so Dad installed a Coleman heater in the back to keep the kids warm until they got to a warmer climate. He added an old Buick radio for them to listen to and built a bench along one side with cushions to sit on. They could lie down on the blanket-covered floor if they wanted to nap. When the occasional squabble broke out, the offenders had to sit up front with Mom and Dad.

This was a vacation on a budget. To take that many kids could cost a fortune. But Mom and Dad knew how to cut corners. They were also not above a little deception to save money. When it came time to pull into a KOA camp, Dad pulled over and put all but two kids in the camper. He drove into the camp, which charged by the person, with only himself, Mom and two kids in the cab of the truck. The gatekeeper would assume there were four people and Dad simply didn't correct him.

All the meals were prepared from the supplies brought along or purchased on the trip. Everybody pitched in and really enjoyed it.

After that first trip, they took winter vacations in Florida most years. On these trips children took responsibility for themselves. If you messed up, you suffered the consequences. Sue and Marie got a lesson in responsibility on one outing.

The family went to Busch Gardens. When they arrived at the park, both Sue and Marie were barefoot and hadn't brought shoes with them. It was a long drive back to the campground where they were staying, and if they went back for shoes, there would not be time to return. Mom decided two girls were not going to ruin the day for everyone else. They spent the day in the truck, in the parking lot while the other kids enjoyed Busch Gardens. Sue and Marie filled the time talking, playing cards and lying around in the truck. They never forgot their shoes again.

As Sue and Marie are telling this story, I am amazed that they accepted their punishment, and are now laughing about it. I ask them why they weren't angry about missing out on the fun. They looked at each other and laughed. "We had fun that day," they said. "Playing cards, talking and just hanging out together was fun." I shook my head as I thought, 'Mom raised some pretty good kids.' In spite of my doubts when I was young, I can now see the wisdom she possessed. I'm sure it was not easy for her to hand out punishment. It would have been much easier to give in, but she had the courage to stick to her convictions when it came to teaching her kids responsibility.

111

# Chapter thirteen

## *Cutting corners*

Mom is feeling better and the nurses and staff at the hospital are more talkative around her. And Mom seems to be enjoying the attention. They ask more questions as they care for her. A question they ask her more than once is "If Mom never worked, how could they afford to raise that many kids on just one person's income?"

They did it by being good at cutting corners. They used every shortcut they could to make ends meet. We were expected to get a job as soon as we were old enough to work. Once we were wage earners, we were responsible for many of our own expenses. We weren't given money to go out with our friends or to buy extras we wanted. We earned our spending money. As we made our own money, we learned to budget and save for the things we really wanted.

For most of us, our first job was babysitting. Not for Mom and Dad. That was considered part of our duties to the family. Our babysitting jobs were for cousins, aunts and uncles, and neighbors with little ones. We had so much experience helping with our younger siblings, babysitting was easy for us. When we started babysitting for relatives Mom insisted we charge no more than two dollars per babysitting job. At that time, 50 to 75 cents an hour was the going rate. Mom said it wasn't fair to overcharge relatives for the service. It was hard to give up a weekend night for just two dollars, but that was the only way we were going to get any spending money.

With our earnings we purchased the things Mom considered extras. Fancy clothes, name brand items we thought were cool, or what Dad called 'store bought' snacks or pop. The refrigerator contents were available to everyone, so if we purchased something, like Pepsi or Mountain Dew, we had better put our name on it, if we expected it to be there when we wanted it. Anything without a name on it was considered community property and we could lose items bought with our hard-earned money.

Mom and Dad saved money many ways. Dad saved money on haircuts for the boys. They did not visit the barbershop. None of my brothers saw the inside of a barbershop until they earned money and could pay for their haircuts. Dad was the family barber. Sunday evening was hair cut night about once every six weeks. Dad set up shop in the kitchen and cut all the boys' hair. As each of his sons hopped up into the makeshift barber chair, (the high chair with a board across the arms) Dad asked the same question, 'Would you like a butch or flat top?' Those were the two hairstyles he felt he had perfected. It really didn't matter which one the boys asked for, the end result was the same, a nearly shaved head. I think Dad learned his barber skills watching the guys in the army. When he was finished, my brothers looked like a bunch of new recruits on the first day of boot camp. The most dreaded haircut was the one each boy received for the first day of school. Through the summer Dad would often skip haircuts, since everybody was busy. By August the boys had full heads of hair; something they could wash with shampoo instead of a bar of soap. But the Sunday before school started each boy got a fresh haircut. Somewhat out of practice, Dad usually made a few mistakes with the clippers. To fix the problem he would cut the rest of the hair to match. None of the boys looked forward to the first haircuts of school year.

Mom had absolutely no talent when it came to hair styling. She didn't have the patience for it. But she did encourage me to give hairdressing a try. My first and only attempt at cutting hair left poor Rose with a disaster the hairdresser could barely fix.

Rose also tried her hand at hairstyling. Sue was her victim. Rose thought, how hard could it be? All she needed was something to follow. Something that would assure the cut was even. She placed a large bowl on Sue's head, and cut around the rim of the bowl, expecting wonderful results. Sue looked like Moe of the Three Stooges. Seeing Sue's hair, Marie was not eager to become the next victim and quickly escaped with her full head of hair.

With no talent for hairstyling in the family, the girls went to the beauty shop each year, just before school started, and before school pictures were taken. Our trip to the hairdresser always included a cut and a perm. We told the hair stylist exactly what we wanted, something like our favorite television star or one if the Mousketeers. Then Mom (who was paying for the hairdo) told them what she wanted. A short cut and a tight perm, it would last longer. She wanted her money's worth. We have many school pictures attesting to this barbaric practice of hair styling on a budget.

We attended Catholic school, where we were required to wear uniforms. We hated them. Mom loved them. With uniforms we looked like everybody else in school (except for the hair), and she didn't have to buy a lot of school clothes. Each girl had a couple of dark blue uniform jumpers, five white blouses, a sweater or two. A new pair of saddle shoes rounded out the outfit. She didn't have to keep up with the latest and coolest styles. The boys had dark blue uniform pants, light blue dress shirts and ties. It made it simple and easy for Mom. When we grew out of our uniform, we passed it down to the next kid (if it wasn't worn out), and if there was someone older than us, theirs was passed down to us.

Our Sunday church clothes and play clothes were handed down, too. Sometimes Mom called us by another kid's name simply because they were wearing an outfit that belonged to someone else just yesterday. We had hand-me-downs from cousins, too. Just because I was the oldest didn't mean I got new clothes all the time.

Going to the shoe store was an expensive trip for Mom. Our school shoes were supposed to make it through the entire school year, unless we outgrew them. When we wanted new shoes Mom would tell us the story about

114

cardboard she put in the bottom of her shoes when she was growing up. We resorted to cardboard a few times ourselves. We each had a pair of dress shoes for church. We took extra special care of those. Every Saturday night we sat around the kitchen table polishing them so they were shining on Sunday morning.

Going shopping for school clothes was an exciting time. New stuff was a luxury and we loved getting new things. One hot August day, after shopping for new school shoes we stopped to visit Mom's sister, Aunt Babe. It was a sweltering, humid August day making the ride in the car miserable. Our cars were never equipped with air-conditioning. When we arrived, hot and sticky from the car ride, our lucky cousins were down at the creek cooling off. Mom said we could go to the creek, but we were not to get in the water, because we weren't staying long. The boys were excited about their new shoes and they wanted to show them off to our cousins, Bud, Richie and Rodney. They grabbed the shoeboxes and ran across the pasture to the creek. The lucky cousins looked cool and comfortable, splashing around in a deep bend of the creek they referred to as the "swimmin' hole." They begged my brothers to join them and cool off a little. The boys knew better than to get in the water. When begging didn't work they dared them to jump in. My brothers, though tempted, resisted. Mom told them we would never get to come to Aunt Babe's again if they got wet and she was known to follow through on her threats. We were leaving right away and Mom didn't want a bunch of soaked kids in her car. As a final attempt to get Dan and David in the water Bud picked up the shiny new school shoes and threw them into the deepest water in the creek, and yelled, "now you have to get in the water to get your shoes."

I never saw Mom so angry with the boys. Those shoes cost a lot of money and there wasn't any extra to replace them. The shoes had to be dried out and were used for the entire year.

Mom also saved S & H green stamps to buy things for around the house. We loved to help her stick all the stamps in the books and dream with her through the Green Stamp catalog. She saved up for small appliances, lamps, dishware, cutlery and dreamed of all the things she could get with her stamps. She also bought and saved FM's. She did her weekly grocery shopping at a local chain store called Fisher Foods. When she purchased her groceries she could buy 10 cents worth of FM's (Fisher Money) for each dollar she spent on groceries. The FM's could be used to buy things in the FM Center, attached to the grocery store. The items were priced lower than the local department stores. Mom bought all her diapers with Fisher Money, and she used a lot of cloth diapers.

No one could stretch food like Mom. She often said, "Some weeks last longer than the grocery's." The meals she made out of very little food were incredible. I sometimes think of the story of the loaves and fishes in the Bible. Jesus fed a huge crowd with just a few loaves of bread and a few fish. It seemed that Mom could do the same on a smaller scale. She had a talent for stretching food. To make soups go farther she added water and salt. If she wanted the milk to last longer she mixed it with powdered milk. To make breads and desserts serve everyone she cut smaller pieces. The meat went farther when Mom used it to make a noodle dish instead of serving it alone. She used a can of pie filling to make two small pies that served more than one large pie. And scrambled eggs made a fine dinner when meat was in short supply. Mom learned many of her short cuts from Grandma Foltz. Grandma fed 16 kids through the depression and knew all the tricks.

Dad saved money by doing repairs and fix-up projects around the house himself. He was a cabinetmaker and carpenter so he was pretty handy with tools. He put tile or laminate floors in many of the rooms. Mom liked them since they were so easy to clean. With that much foot traffic, the floors needed mopped three times a week. But she really wanted carpet in the bedrooms. My Aunt Lori, one of Mom's older sisters, showed Mom how she did it in her house. She got carpet samples, those pieces of carpet the stores used to help customers pick out types and colors of carpet. The carpet stores throw them away or sell them cheaply. Aunt Lori bought some and glued them onto her floors with carpet glue. It really didn't look bad. A checkerboard floor. So Mom bought some carpet samples and did our bedrooms. That's carpeting on a budget. We all thought it was great, better than the tile floor. But when friends came over they thought it was pretty funny. We didn't care, as long as the floor was warm on our bare feet when we got up in the morning.

The houses we lived in had coal furnaces. On cold winter nights the fire in the furnace got low from lack of fuel and by morning the house had a definite chill. It felt so good to snuggle under the covers to stay warm. But if you didn't get up first, you didn't get a register downstairs. We hurried down to claim a register when Dad stoked up the furnace. Standing on the register as the hot air from the furnace ballooned my nightgown out around me felt great on a cold winter morning. Other kids begged to share the one-foot by two-foot piece of heaven blowing out hot air. But if I got up first it was mine; till Mom heard the begging and made us share. Oh, it was great to have the heat if only for a little while.

With a family our size we were always short of chairs in the living room. With that many people wanting to watch "Bonanza" or "The Ed Sullivan Show" seating was at a premium. Everyone wanted to watch those shows and others favorites like "Top Cat" and "The Flintstones." Even Dad watched with us. There were about eight seats in the living room and the rule was first come, first served. Except in the case of Mom and Dad, they got first choice. Once all the chairs and sofa were taken, you were stuck with the floor. The boys liked the floor. Some of our early television sets in the 50"s and 60"s stood on legs, and the boys liked to lie on the floor and put their feet under the TV. There was a hot air register under there and they had toasty feet in the winter while they got a close up look at the screen. They ignored Grandma's warning that they would get 'radiation poisoning' if they stayed that close to a TV set. If we got up from our chair for any reason we lost our seat. That was the rule. It didn't matter why we vacated our chair; we could not claim it when we returned. For this reason, few kids even left the room during commercial breaks. Bathroom breaks were kept to a minimum and if we had a good seat we didn't even get up for a snack. We would con some little kid into getting it for us.

When my husband and I first started dating he came over one evening and wanted to walk across the room. He stood there and asked "How do you get through here?'

I replied, "Just step over them".

"But what if I step on one of them?" was his concern.

"Don't worry," I assured him. "They won't move." And they didn't move, or notice that anyone had stepped over them.

Dad had picked up the habit of smoking cigarettes as a young man. He got really hooked in the service during World War II. But cigarettes were an expense. Dad saved money even on this vice by rolling his own cigarettes. We loved to watch him roll them. He taught the boys the craft. It was quite an art form. If the cigarettes had too little tobacco, they would be gone in a few puffs. If they had too much tobacco, Dad couldn't draw the smoke through them to enjoy the cigarette. There needed to have just the right amount of tobacco in each cigarette. Then he rolled the white paper around the tobacco, moistened the edge of the paper where it met to seal it and let it dry. The boys got pretty good at getting it just right.

There wasn't a lot of money for doctor and dentist appointments, so they were on an as-needed basis only. We didn't have regular doctor or dental checkups with that many of us. We thought it was great at the time. We all got our baby shots and physicals required for school, plus a trip to the doctor if we were sick. We had a family doctor named Dr. Hendershot. That name alone can make you dread the appointment.

We never purchased a new car. It was Dad's philosophy that a used car, in good condition, was as good as new. Most of our cars were station wagons, so everyone could get in the car. Even with a nine-passenger station wagon there were not enough seats. The older kids had a little one on their lap for most family outings. For years I arrived at every destination with a wrinkled skirt, the result of a squirming little boy sitting on my lap.

We never wasted anything. "Waste not, want not" according to Mom. Finding a use for things some people would discard was a necessary function. Growing up during the Depression and then living through World War II taught my parents to conserve. There were many things we didn't have to buy. For example, cotton balls came free in aspirin bottles. Any product fastened with a rubber band provided free rubber bands. String was saved and tied to the loose end of the ball of string in the 'junk' drawer in the kitchen. The junk drawer contained anything that might be useful in the future. Loose nails, screws, washers, candle stubs, partially burned birthday cake candles, and used batteries rolled around the bottom of the drawer, along with small parts that came off of who knows what machine or appliance. My mother's button collection in her Niagara Falls souvenir tin, kept in the hutch, was outstanding. There was every kind of button imaginable. When a piece of clothing was finally worn out, all the buttons were cut off and saved before it could be thrown out. Who knew when you would need that exact button? I was a teenager before I realized you could actually buy buttons in the store.

Mom's sisters were just as thrifty. Aunt Lori told Mom that if she bought bath soap ahead, unwrapped the bars, and stored them for a while, they would harden and last longer. We had a drawer full of unwrapped soap bars, hardening. Ivory soap was Mom's favorite; it was inexpensive and would float so she could find it in the tub full of little kids. Bathing the kids was an assembly line process with Mom washing and me drying and getting them into their PJ's. With the haircuts Dad gave the boys we saved on shampoo, they washed their 'flat tops or crew cuts' with a bar of soap.

Saving and cutting corners allowed Mom and Dad to make sure we had the necessities: food, clothing, shelter, and education along with the few little extras they could afford.

Looking out the hospital window I can see palm trees swaying in the breeze. Right now I would love to take a walk in the lovely breeze with the sun shining on my face. Someone suggests we go out to the local Wendy's for lunch. A break from the hospital sounds great. I'll take a walk around the hospital when we get back to refresh my mind and relax a little. We give Mom a kiss goodbye and tell her to get some rest. We will be back later in the afternoon. She looks tired. She could use a break from us, and a nap.

# Chapter Fourteen

## *Tricks*

A quick lunch and a walk around the hospital grounds is a restful break. Mom looks refreshed from her nap and she wants to visit with everyone. Mom is happiest when her kids are around her. She loves to talk for hours. She's a great storyteller and doesn't hesitate to tell you when you have some facts wrong as you're telling the story. She always says she should write a book about raising so many kids. It would be very different from "Cheaper by the Dozen." (A book title that irritated her.) "They are not cheaper by the dozen," she says. Her story would be more factual. She considered "Cheaper by the Dozen" a fantasy. "Although," she said, "Real life with 15 kids is never dull."

When there are so many kids living together a pecking order evolves. Those with the leadership qualities will naturally become the ones looked up to and followed by the more timid ones. The older boys often took advantage of the little ones. Sometimes I wonder how the younger boys put up with the tricks played on them by their older brothers.

Gerard, three years younger than David, was an easy target for Dan and David. He would believe anything they told him. Gullible should be his middle name. On warm summer nights on the farm, with the windows open, we lay in bed, unable to sleep in the summer heat, listening to the night sounds. There was no traffic noise, or neighborhood sounds. There was just the quiet of the country and the sound of night creatures moving about. One such creature was a bird we called a Whip-O-Will. The name came from the sound it made at dusk. Dan and David lay in bed listening one night when Gerard made the mistake of asking why the bird was calling repeatedly. In their best big brother teaching voices they convinced Gerard the bird was calling him and he should go out and find it. Gerard said he was afraid to go out after dark by himself; so they told him if he didn't go to the bird, it would come for him. Dan and David lay in bed snickering as poor Gerard cowered in fear of the imagined bird of prey. After several nights of trying to be brave, the little guy finally cried for Mom. When she came into the room and discovered Dan and David tormenting their little brother, she made them get up and go out to the shed and throw rocks on the tin roof and scare the birds away.

Dan enjoyed tormenting the younger kids. He never physically tortured anyone. It was always psychological. He convinced some of the younger kids they were adopted and could be sent back at any time. He made some believe they were robots, controlled by others. He was pretty persuasive.

David was his favorite victim. One chilly fall day the boys were working in the barn; David throwing hay down from the hayloft to feed the cows and Dan putting it in feeders. David was getting tired and lost his grip on the pitchfork handle. It came flying down with the hay. Dan started screaming as if the pitchfork had stabbed him. David couldn't see from above, but from the screaming he heard he was convinced his brother was dying and he had killed him. Just then, Dan suddenly became perfectly quiet, as if he'd died. David really did want to kill him when he ran down to discover Dan laughing hysterically. There just happened to be a baseball bat handy. It's a good thing Dan could outrun David or he might not be here today.

The kids were in big trouble if Dan knew they had done something wrong. If they had done something they could be punished for, Dan would hold it over their head until they had something on him to cancel his out. Like the time Rose broke a glass jar in the granary. We were not permitted to play in the granary, but it was a fun place we just couldn't resist. There were bins of oats and wheat for feeding the animals and playing in them was a blast, until we stirred up so much grain dust we couldn't breathe. Why

Rose had a glass jar in there I don't know, but she dropped it and it broke into several pieces. Dan witnessed the accident. He helped her clean up the mess as he warned her that if Dad found out she was in big trouble. Glass in the grain would kill the animals if they ate it and that was her fault. She was his slave for months. The poor girl was at his mercy. She did some of his chores, shared her treats with him, and waited on him hand and foot.

Rose was an easy victim, almost as gullible as Gerard. On a sunny summer afternoon he convinced her to taste milkweed. When broken, the stem of a milkweed plant oozes an extremely bitter white substance. It tastes horrible. Dan convinced Rose to try the milkweed, telling her how sweet it was. As soon as she put the stem in her mouth she knew she'd made a mistake. Dan rolled on the ground laughing as she ran for the garden hose as fast as she could.

All the kids joined in a favorite practical joke around the farm involving the electric milk cooler. We milked by hand and poured the milk through a strainer into old-fashioned milk cans. When the milking was finished each morning and evening the cans were placed in a big metal cooler filled with cold water to be picked up by the milk truck that came a couple of times a week. Since we did not qualify for Grade A milk we sold to a candy factory. To qualify as Grade A, and get a highest price, we would need milking equipment and expensive upgrades to the barn, so Dad settled for selling to a candy company. We loved it when the candy company put a gift pack of six different candy bars in one of the empty cans on holidays. What a treat! But 6 candy bars were not enough for our family so Mom cut them in half. We didn't care as we savored our half.

Back to the cooler. It was electric and must have had a short in it. Sometimes when we touched it we got shocked. We loved to take the city cousins to the barn and get them to touch the cooler. The electric fence didn't work as well because they suspected they would get shocked. We got a laugh watching their faces when they touched the cooler.

Playing tricks on each other wasn't reserved for the boys. The girls weren't angels by any means. Everyone loved to scare another kid in the dark. Once Jerry came up the stairs in the dark when the light bulb had burned out. Marie, Sue and Jane were in their bedroom. The only light in the hall came form a night-light at the top of the stairs. Just as Jerry walked past the girls' bedroom door, Jane slowly wormed her hand out the door, just under the night-light. All Jerry could see in the dim light was a white hand seemingly suspended in thin air. He ran screaming down the dark stairway as the girls lay on their beds laughing.

Mom enjoyed pulling practical jokes on the kids. We seldom had chocolate candy. It was reserved for Easter and other special occasions. Mom's favorite joke was to take an unsuspecting kid aside, and whispered that she had a treat for them. They could not tell anyone else. Then, she gave them a piece of bitter baking chocolate. She loved that joke. I think she pulled it 15 times.

She was a determined woman. When Mom put her mind to something you could not stop her. She started projects and got the kids involved, whether they wanted to join in or not. Our house on the farm was on a hill, overlooking an empty field and a pond. We planted a large garden at the top of the field near the house. A low wall of stone separated the yard and field from each other. The wall was covered with vines and weeds and was falling apart. It looked awful. Mom thought, with the help of the kids, she could clear away all the weeds and vines, and carry away the stones. She set to work with her crew of little helpers on a hot summer day. She tore the vines out by the roots as we carried away the stones. It was hot, backbreaking work and she often used the back of her hand to wipe the sweat from her forehead and eyes as she worked. All afternoon we carried rocks down the hill to the area near the pond. After a hard day's work the wall was gone and the area looked much better. Mom gathered up her kids and tools just before suppertime and went in to wash up. Her face began to itch as she cooked the meal. The next morning it was swollen.

Within a day her face was so puffed up she couldn't open her eyes. Her hands were covered with raw blisters. The vines on the wall had been poison ivy and she had been pulling it out and rubbing it on her face all day. Several of the kids had a rash, too. Dad brought Grandma Foltz down to the farm to help with the kids until Mom could see again. We went through several bottles of pink calamine lotion. Mom looked terrible, swollen with pink lotion covering her hands and face. The littlest ones were afraid of her. We said some special prayers at bedtime until she healed.

We're tired. It's incredible how drained I feel when I haven't done anything for days. Stress and this feeling of helplessness overwhelm me. As I look around at the others I notice everyone looks spent. We're ready for a good night's sleep. Tomorrow will be our last day with Mom. I am not looking forward to the long drive home. And I don't really want to leave.

# Chapter Fifteen

## *Back to Ohio*

Now that Mom is recovering, most of us must go home. We have families and jobs waiting for us. We don't want to leave but there is really no choice. Dad is a little reluctant to let us go. He knows we need to leave, but how is he ever going to take care of Mom? According to the doctors, she has a long convalescence ahead of her. It will be a quite some time before she can do things for herself.

After a family conference, we decide to go back to Ohio, leaving Rose to help Dad. She doesn't have a job to return to, and her kids are old enough to take care of themselves for a while. So she will stay.

Rose cries at the prospect of staying without the rest of us. She feels abandoned, and nervous about helping Dad take responsibility for Mom's care. But she'll stay because that's her nature. That's Rose.

Rose was an unhappy child. She never seemed to get enough of Mom's love and attention. Mom said she had middle child syndrome even though she was not the middle child.

She constantly irritated the rest of us. She called everyone a 'butt' whenever she was mad, which was most of the time. Calling the other kids 'butt' was as close as she dared come to swearing. That would get her a mouth full of soap. I am four and a half years older than Rose. I didn't understand her when we were children, and that didn't help me to accept her behavior. There were boys on either side of her in the birth order, so she didn't have a close sister.

For years she tagged along with Dan and David trying to prove she was every bit as strong and daring as they were. That would have been a challenge for any girl with

126

brothers to compete with. But it was really hard with Dan and David tormenting her unmercifully. They challenged her to some pretty dangerous stunts and she came through every time. They played tricks on her that bordered on cruel. Like getting her to taste milkweed.

Dan and David tired of a little sister tagging along and tried anything to get rid of her. They often pelted her with apples when she tried to climb up to the 'boys only' tree house.

In her constant bid for attention she would push the others until our frustration level was so high we attacked and got her down on the floor. She cried and made us feel bad, then when we let her go she would get up and laugh. It was infuriating. Growing up with Rose was never dull.

But as an adult she is the one we can rely on. She is always there when anyone needs her. Mom always says "Rose will give you the shirt off her back if you need it."

So Rose would stay and help. We reluctantly said our goodbyes. Mom's weeks of recuperating turned into months. Rose went home and Dad and Jane became the principal caregivers. As spring nears Mom fears she won't get back north for the summer. The thought of missing her annual trip seems to help her recover. She sets a goal of getting to Ohio and tells her doctor about it. He recommends she stay home, but Mom is determined. She calls Rose and asks her to arrange for a doctor in Ohio. She has her medical records sent to the new doctor. Every year Dad and Mom take two or three days to travel to Ohio in the motor home. This year she realizes she cannot spend that much time on the road, even with the conveniences of a house on wheels. So she decides to fly to Ohio. Dad has no desire to fly. Mom's afraid to fly alone, so Sue flies to Florida to accompany her back to Ohio. This gives Sue a chance to visit Jane, Vince, Tim, Andy and Ed for a few days. Dad kisses Mom goodbye as he puts her and Sue on the plane in Naples. He plans to leave for Ohio in the motor home the next day.

As the plane taxis to the runway, Mom sits in her window seat, ecstatic that she is actually going back to Ohio. She can't wait to take off. As she glances out the window of the plane, on her first flight, she sees the runway they will be using for takeoff. She notices an alligator sunning himself on the concrete. Mom points it out to Sue as they taxi on to the end of the runway. Then they just sit there in the plane for several minutes. Mom is getting nervous. Why aren't they taking off? She has said her prayers asking for a safe flight and is ready to go. She wants to be airborne and on her way to Ohio. Asking a flight attendant about the delay, she is told about the alligator on the runway. He's contentedly sunning himself and is in no hurry to move. They can't take off until he leaves. Airport security finally sends a truck and driver to encourage the animal to leave the warm concrete. After some coaxing he slowly lumbers away and the plane is cleared to take off. With a sigh of relief Mom is airborne and on her way to her kids in Ohio.

Rose and I pick Mom and Sue up in Cleveland Hopkins Airport. I cannot hide my alarm when I see her. She is so small and frail. She has changed tremendously in less than six months. Her skin is thin and translucent and she looks much older than her mid 60"s. The airline provides a wheelchair at the gate, and we take her to my car, as she happily chats about her flight. I settle her in the front seat of my car as Sue and Rose get in the back. She is nauseous from the plane ride and the hour-long car ride isn't going to help. I feel so bad for her. But she smiles, happy just to be here.

In spite of her fatigue she is excited to be back in Ohio. She has questions about everyone and talks about seeing the kids and grandchildren again. As I drive, I keep glancing over at her, sitting in the seat beside me. She looks so frail. I have to keep reminding myself that this is the same woman who left Ohio last fall, in apparent good health.

I am relieved to get to Rose's house, where Mom is staying until Dad arrives in a few days. After the long flight and the car ride from the airport she needs to lie down. Rose is excited to have some time with her. As we settle her in I realize she is not going to bounce back from this illness. I go home and look up all the information I can find on congestive heart failure. I wish I hadn't. After reading up on the subject, I realize we are at the beginning of the end. I am determined to make the most of what time we have left.

We have the entire summer to enjoy Mom's company as much as we can. We visit Springwood as often as possible. Mom is well enough to enjoy our visits but needs to stay close to the house most of the time. We gather on the screened-in porch at the campsite and spend hours talking and laughing. The conversation turns to our adventures while growing up. Mom sits in her favorite rocking chair or the wooden porch swing and enjoys the company of her children. The grandkids come along and run to the swimming pool across the road. Some bring toys and bicycles with them, to play on the hot summer days.

One of the wonderful things about such a large family is the fun you have together. Watching the children run and play around the campsite reminds us of the many happy hours we spent playing together. Mom and Dad were often right there with us, joining in the fun.


Bicycles and tricycles were always around as we were growing up. Everyone had one. They were seldom new, but we didn't care. As long as they had handlebars, wheels and pedals we were happy. We didn't even need a seat. If a bike was missing a seat you could ride standing up. Mom loved to ride a bike and could be seen many summer days riding with the kids. She said it was good exercise and made her feel like a kid again. She especially enjoyed the bicycle built for two they won in a contest when they bought the campsite. They rode together around the park like two kids. That is, when they could get it away from the kids.

There are perils to all activities and more than one kid got a foot caught in the spokes or a pant leg tangled in the chain. Bike accidents were common. But Mom told us to pick ourselves up or put a band-aid on the cuts and scrapes. 'You'll live' was as close as we got to sympathy when we did something stupid.

An early game of baseball marked the start of spring. A baseball diamond could be any size depending on how much space we had to lay it out. But when we moved to Louisville we used the airport runway as a baseball field. The grass runway of Yoder's airport bordered the back of our property. We set up a ball diamond at the end of the runway using rocks for bases. Mr. Yoder didn't mind as long as we picked the rocks up from the runway at the end of the game. Baseball games were fun, but with a team made up of kids ranging in age from sixteen to two, special rules were required. There was no rulebook. We made them up as we went along. The pitcher stood closer to home plate when the little ones were up to bat, giving them a chance to hit the ball. No one hurried to catch or tag them out. If anyone didn't like the rules they didn't have to play. If someone wasn't happy about the game and wanted to quit when they didn't get their way, Mom said, "go ahead and quit." She'd tell us, "One monkey don't make no show."

When he built the runway Mr. Yoder made a deal with my brothers. He would take them up in his plane if they picked the rocks off the runway and piled them to the side. When they had accumulated a few piles of rocks, he taxied to the edge of our property and invited some of the kids to join him for a plane ride. Two at a time. They excitedly ran to tell Mom they were taking off. Dan and David were first to go up. Dan was in the front seat with Mr. Yoder and David sat in the back. Mr. Yoder gave the boys a thrill doing some loops and dives. After few minutes Dan turned around to see David wide eyed, hanging on for dear life. Dan was nauseous, but he wasn't going to let that ruin his ride. Mr. Yoder allowed him to hold the yoke and told him he was actually flying the plane. He asked Dan to take them home; Dan couldn't tell him which way was home. Mr. Yoder laughed and showed Dan how to find landmarks on the ground to tell where you were. It was quite an experience for a couple of young boys.

The only flying the boys had experienced before riding in Mr. Yoder's small plane was flying kites. Kites were inexpensive and a project we could do together. Dad enjoyed kite flying when we lived in Florida. Nancy and I would sit on the sandy beach on warm days watching Dad fly kites over the ocean. We watched until the kite was so small you could hardly see it. It was amazing to two little girls that Dad could do that.

In Ohio, big empty fields were wonderful for an afternoon of kite flying. On a windy spring day kids with brightly colored kites competed for Dad's assistance in getting their kite airborne. Was there too much tail? Not enough tail? Were we letting out the string too fast or too slow? These were questions Dad asked each little pilot if they wondered why their kite just wouldn't fly. Kite flying training was serious business on those windy spring days. There was a wonderful feeling of power when our kite was finally up and flying. It was worth running through the soggy fields getting wet feet, cold noses and numb fingers.

Like many families in the 50's and 60's we loved the Sunday drive. On a beautiful sunny Sunday we climbed into the car to just drive. After the usual arguments over the window seats, off we went. Dad stopped at the filling station, where an attendant in a white shirt with his name sewn over the pocket bounced out of the station, smiled and said, "Can I fill it up?" Dad said, "Just a dollar's worth, please". At 25 cents a gallon we got pretty far on a dollar's worth. We usually had no particular destination. Dad drove leisurely around the countryside until the kids got restless. We sat in back of the station wagon trying to spot an ice cream stand, so we could beg for a cone. Or, when we stopped at a gas station, we hoped to get a GetUp or orange Nehi from the soft drink machine. We sat in the car, with the windows down, trying to drink our soda as fast as Dad drank his. Then we ran over to the wooden crates beside the machine, and put our bottles in the slots before we hurried back to the car. A Sunday drive without a stop for a treat was a disappointment. Everyone behaved in the car or Dad wouldn't stop. Anyone who acted up and caused us to miss out on a treat answered to the rest of us when we got home.

Roller-skating was a favorite family activity. Everyone loved to skate, except me. I spent most of my time at the rink getting picked up off the floor by the rink attendants. I went to school with the boy whose father owned the rink, and he was the one usually picking me up off the floor I was embarrassed.

The local rink, Cholley's, featured family night on Sunday. The entire family got in for one low price. Our family really made out on that offer. Dad loaded us into the car and drove over to the rink right after supper. Mom often stayed home with the babies and Dad supervised the skaters. I offered to stay home so Mom could go. I wanted to escape the embarrassment of being picked up off the floor, but Mom and Dad insisted I needed the exercise and wanted me to join in the family fun. When the babies were old enough to skate, Mom went too. Since my parents both loved skating, this family activity was a favorite of theirs.

In the 60's the local rink held teen dances on Saturday nights. Dan and I preferred the rink on Saturday night when our friends were there enjoying the DJ or local garage bands. As a teenager, family night was not cool. So Dan and I begged to go on Saturday night to dance instead of skate. Once we got there, we split up and hung out with our own friends. How embarrassing is it to spend Saturday night with your brother?

The older we got the less we enjoyed togetherness with the younger kids. We wanted to get out with kids our own age and enjoy some freedom. Mom and Dad were reluctant to let go. The older kids had to pave the way for the others. Letting go of the kids meant losing control and risking that they would make wrong choices. Not easy for my parents to do. But as we grew, Mom and Dad had no choice but to let go and pray things would go well for us.

Every summer we have a family reunion. It may seem silly to call our annual picnic a reunion; we're together quite a bit throughout the year. But we wanted to start a tradition so our children and their children would get together at least once a year to celebrate family. Mom's family has an annual reunion that has been held every summer for over 80 years and still going. We hope ours will last as long. Mom cannot take an entire day away from home. She needs to rest in the afternoon. So Jerry, who is in charge of the reunion this year, booked the pavilion at Springwood. Mom can enjoy the picnic dinner, go back to the trailer for a nap, and come back to the reunion. I'm grateful that Jerry was so thoughtful and we are able to have the reunion with Mom there. She wouldn't want to miss it. Family gatherings are important to her.

# Chapter Sixteen

## *Grandma Foltz*

Mom called early this morning with the sad news that Grandma Foltz passed away. Mom is understandably upset but as Grandma would tell us, "It was time." She was 96 years old. She had arranged her own funeral many years ago. It will be at the Wackerly Funeral Home in Canton, where Grandpa's was held. Nancy's was there, too. Her funeral Mass will be at St. Peters, same as Nancy's. I tell Mom I will be at the calling hours and ask her if she needs anything. "No," she says. She will be all right. She just wants to be sure we will all be there for Grandma.

When I arrive at the funeral home there is quite a crowd. The day after Grandma died, the local newspaper, the Canton Repository, ran an article on the first page of the second section. She left an amazing 270 decedents. That's quite a legacy. I can barely move in the room adjoining the viewing area, it is so crowded. It takes quite some time to get to the casket. I'm grateful this is not the same room where Nancy's viewing had been held. As I kneel at the casket I say a prayer, as much for Mom as for Grandma. It's hard to believe it has been six years since Grandma's 90th birthday party. What a wonderful celebration that was. She maintained her independence as long as she could. But the last several years she lived with Aunt Babe and Uncle Roy. I walk away from the casket to greet some of my aunts and uncles. But mostly I'm watching Mom. She is in her element. Surrounded by family. She looks tiny and frail in the new dress she bought for the funeral. It's a black flowered dress with puff sleeves and a white collar. It seems too big for her, making her look even smaller.

She and her sisters and brothers are chatting and laughing together. For just a minute I think, "Isn't this a

funeral? Shouldn't they be crying?" But I know Gra
would never have stood for that. She had a good long
She lived for her family and believed in the grace of
He knew what was best, and her time had come.

Mom was very much like her mother. They l
loved their children unconditionally. Grandma had 16. T
both fervently believed in God and his goodness in bless
them with a wonderful life, even if he also sent some tri
They had both buried a little child. Mom lost Nancy a
Grandma lost a little girl named Helen. Baby Hel
contracted Whooping Cough and died in Grandma's arms
she rocked her in front of the coal stove. She was only thr
months old. That was in 1929; Mom was four years ol
then.

Grandma was born Blanche Hinkle on May 5, 189
but she was really a Marchand. That was her mother'
maiden name and Grandma was like the other Marchand
woman, very strong willed. She met and fell in love with
Emerson Foltz. Emerson was not a satisfactory husband in
the eyes of Grandma's mother. He had contracted polio as a
child and was considered a cripple. Besides that, he was a
house painter. Grandma's mother did not consider house
painting a fitting profession for her youngest daughter'
husband. And she was convinced that their children woul
be cripples, like Grandpa. But, being every bit as stron
willed as her mother, Grandma married Grandpa in spite
her protest.

Grandma's father talked Grandpa into attendi
barber school and paid the tuition. A barber was a bet
occupation than a painter for their daughter's husband. I
Grandpa really did not like the job and didn't stick with it.

Grandma was an independent woman, which w
good thing since Grandpa liked to drink some. He par
of the "painter's medicine" as alcohol was sometimes ca
And painting houses is not a year-round occupation in C
So money was always short. Grandma worked outsid
home most of her life. She was a cook in many o

restaurants in Canton. She worked at night so she could care for her constantly expanding family in the daytime. After a while she had some built-in babysitters and took some day jobs.

When I attended Central Catholic High School, Grandma was on the cleaning staff. I often saw her in the halls and snuck in a wave or stopped to talk, if I had time between classes. I wasn't happy she was there when she sometimes reported things to my Mom I really didn't want her to know. Every morning, Mass was held in the school gym. Most mornings I attended, but occasionally I hung out in the girl's restroom with friends, trying different makeup or talking about boys, instead of going to Mass. And I rolled up the waist of my uniform skirt so the hem fell above my knees, which was strictly forbidden. Every once in a while, the nuns ordered us to kneel beside our desks, to check if our skirt hem touched the floor. If it didn't we were in trouble. With mine rolled up I could quickly roll it down to make sure the hem was low enough. Then, after inspection, I rolled it back up. Or I snuck off to the grotto in the morning before class to meet my boyfriend. The boys and girls were separated in the building. Boys attended classes on a different side of the building. The only time we were together was in the gym during Mass or assemblies. Even then we were kept on opposite sides of the auditorium. Sometimes Grandma mentioned to Mom that she didn't see me at Mass and Mom wanted to know why. But mostly Grandma was cool. We could talk to her. I loved to stay at her house.

Pop Foltz, as Grandpa was known, died in 1962. He was 69 years old. Each of the grandchildren took turns staying with Grandma for several weekends after Grandpa passed away. I remember my weekend stay with my cousin Carolyn. We slept on the foldout couch and stayed up late, eating chocolate-covered graham crackers and milk until we were sick.

Like Mom, Grandma was always there for her children. She spent many weeks at our house, watching us

when Mom went to the hospital to have a new baby. She stayed on and helped Mom until the baby was a few weeks old. She went to anyone's house if there was an illness or tragedy and someone needed her. With a family that large, she was always occupied.

Grandma loved to read and enjoyed religious books and magazines. She also subscribed to the *Reader's Digest*. Mom didn't have the extra money to spend on magazines when I was growing up. Grandma knew I loved to read so she brought her *Reader's Digest* to me when she was finished with them. How I looked forward to those magazines.

When Mom lived in Ohio she picked Grandma up every Friday morning and took her shopping for groceries. They often went to lunch or to visit one of Mom's sisters. Mom enjoyed spending time with her mother.

Missing her mother was one of the reasons Mom came back to Ohio each summer when Nancy was little. When Mom and Dad moved to Florida permanently, Mom found she still missed her mother as much as she did when she was young. On their first trip back to Ohio she convinced Grandma Foltz to go back to Florida with them. Grandma consented to go, only to find when she got there she had to share a bedroom with Jane. Jane was not any happier than Grandma, but the house only had three bedrooms. The younger boys shared an even smaller room than Jane had. Jane hung a life-size poster of Clark Gable in a black tuxedo on the back of her bedroom door. When Grandma woke during the night she saw the poster and in her sleepiness, just for a moment, thought someone was standing there. Jane refused to take the poster down. After all, this was her room and she would keep it the way she wanted it.

Grandma and Mom sat on the front porch in the warm Florida winter afternoons and talked for hours. Grandma was 86 that winter, but her mind was sharp. Mom could ask her anything about the hundreds of relatives and Grandma had a story to tell. Grandma enjoyed walking in the back yard and picking citrus fruit off the trees. She got around pretty well using a cane. They went shopping and out to lunch like they did in Ohio, but Grandma tired more easily then.

Grandma spent just the one winter with Mom in Florida. She wanted to return to Ohio to be near most of her children and grandchildren. Mom had to settle for seeing her in the summer, when she returned to Ohio each year.

I walk with Mom to the car after calling hours. She takes my arm and leans over to whisper that an old boyfriend of hers saw the article in the paper and came to pay his respects. She was actually giggling. This is the first I've heard about this old boyfriend. She tells me they dated before she met Dad. She's so flattered that after all these years he wanted to see her. He asked if she is happy, and wanted to know all about her life, where she had been and what she had done. He had married, too. But his wife had passed away. As I look at her I see a sparkle in her eye and I can imagine her as a young woman, being courted by more than one young man. It's a picture of Mom I had never imagined before. I only thought of her as Mom, inseparable from Dad, not as an individual.

As Dad approaches us, she put her finger to her lips to indicate she doesn't want him to know. I am grateful to the gentleman for giving her such joy on this sad day.

The next morning we attend the funeral Mass at beautiful St. Peters church in Canton. It reminds me of the many Sundays I attended church here with my parents when I was small. Burial is at St. Peters Cemetery near Nancy's grave. After the priest finished the graveside prayers, Dan and I walk together to Nancy's grave to say a prayer. There is no stone marking her resting place, but we know right where it is. Even without walking it off.

## Chapter Seventeen

### *Growing up*

Mom spent time in the hospital this summer. Her lungs are filling with fluid quite often and pneumonia is a problem. On a beautiful July Sunday after attending 12:00 Mass at St. Louis, I go to the hospital to visit Mom for the afternoon. She is feeling pretty good today, and is very talkative. Mom can talk for hours. It's her favorite thing to do. I really enjoy our visit and talking with her, it is time I can have alone with Mom. With so many siblings time alone with Mom is rare. When I arrive Sue is just leaving. I have the whole afternoon to spend with her. We talk about so many things, including raising kids. Mom says raising kids keeps a person young. It kept her active and with so many children to take care of, she didn't have time to sit around feeling down. As far as she is concerned raising kids is the best thing you can do with your life. She tells me again, as she had many times as I was growing up, "God never gives you more than you can handle." Whenever we complained about a burden or problem, Mom would repeat that phrase. I ask her if that includes raising teenagers.

As the kids grew up and became teenagers Mom had a whole new set of adventures to contend with. It was the early 60's when the first of us entered our teens. I turned 13 in 1961, and the last of the group, Ed, turned 20 in 1987. That is an astonishing total of 26 years with teenagers in the house. And not just one or two at a time; there could be several at once. Mom should be considered an expert on the subject of teenagers. Up until the time some of us started high school we pretty much stayed at home and spent our time together under her protective wing. We had plenty of playmates right in our house. But as the kids learned to drive, they discovered independence.

Neither Mom nor Dad was blessed with patience. Without patience, teaching us to drive was a challenge. The older boys learned on the farm, driving the tractors and pickup trucks in the fields. The transition to street driving was easy for them. However, I was another story. I was the first to get my coveted temps. It was a proud spring day when I came home with that piece of paper. I couldn't wait to get behind the wheel of a car. I had never driven on the farm, but how hard could it be if my little brothers could do it? After all Dan drove all the time. If he could do it, so could I. Finally, after a few days of begging, Mom consented to give me my first driving lesson. Sitting behind the wheel, listening to her explain how everything worked, was a bore. I just wanted to make the car move. As she explained the brake, clutch, gas pedal, gearshift and steering wheel, I was about jumping out of the seat. My response to everything she said was "Yeah, Yeah." I thought she would never stop talking.

The car was an old station wagon. It seems all our cars were old station wagons when I was young. There was no power anything. No power steering or power brakes. I'm all of five feet tall and my feet didn't even reach the pedals. We moved the seat as far forward as possible, and I inched up to the very edge of the seat. All this time Mom was explaining how to use my left foot for the clutch and my right foot for the gas and brake. I was nearly exploding with excitement as I practiced pushing on the three pedals. I was about to drive. This was incredible. That is, if Mom would just stop talking long enough for me to get started. I was finally allowed to turn the key and start the car. I sat there in the driveway with the motor running. Now we were getting somewhere. The car was pointed up the driveway, away from the main street. There was about 75 feet of straight drive and then a sharp right, down a small hill, past the barn, and out onto a little-used dirt road. I wouldn't be going the other way, onto a paved street with more of a chance of encountering real traffic. I put the car in drive with my foot on the clutch and brake. As I took my foot off the brake, eased off the clutch and applied pressure to the gas pedal, the car lurched forward, causing me to lose footing on both pedals, and the car stalled. As a typical teenager, my reaction was one of disgust. What was the matter with this stupid car? It worked for Mom.

"OK," Mom said, "let's try again. Start the car again and very gently press on the gas as you slowly let out the clutch."

Great!! Now the car is actually moving slowly up the drive, with me grinning like an idiot behind the wheel. This is great!! I glanced out the driver's side window at the collection of little onlookers who have gathered to watch the momentous occasion. They were enthusiastically waving, as if I were leaving on an extended trip instead of a short way up the drive. We were approaching the turn in the drive, but I'm so busy looking cool for the little ones I didn't realize, I'm the one who needs to steer this thing. Finally, Mom gets my attention by shouting, "Turn! Turn! Turn!" I slowly turn the wheel. But the wheel didn't turn as easily as it did for Dad and Mom. There is something wrong with the steering. I pull with all my might, but the car barely turned. By this time we were approaching the side of the barn. I was looking at the steering wheel, willing it to turn, instead of watching where I was going. We were no longer on the driveway, although I was not aware of it and Mom was screaming, "Stop! Stop!" at the top of her lungs. As I finally look up from the steering wheel I saw, directly in front of me, the huge side of the barn. My foot slammed on the brake and Mom shot forward into the dashboard as the car stalled. There were no seat-belts in old 1950s' station wagons. Poor Mom was without any protection. That was the end of the lesson. Mom was convinced I wanted her dead, and killing her during a driving lesson was how I would do it. I sat there in the stalled car, with little siblings dancing around outside the car door, laughing hysterically about the whole thing. I couldn't believe driving required you to do so many things at the same time. How can you work three different pedals with only two feet, watch where you are going, and work a steering wheel that would hardly move, all at the same time? At that moment, I lost my desire to drive. I decided to let the temporary permit expire. Mom had no problem with that decision; she was not interested in any more attempts to teach me to drive. She told me to wait until Dan got his license and he could teach me. What an embarrassing idea. Having a little brother teach you to drive.

Dan was the first to drive and buy a car. He got a job at T N T Television, a local appliance store, and earned enough for a '58 Chevy Delray and insurance. It cost him $450.00. He had a loan, cosigned by Dad. Dad said boys needed to drive so they could get to jobs and run errands. It really was not necessary for girls to drive. That was a little outdated attitude even in the early 1960s. Boys also needed a car to date girls. Dating was much easier if you had your own car. Picking up a girl in Dad's work car, another old station wagon full of tools, was not cool. Before getting his own car, Dan would wash and wax the old station wagon every Friday night to use over the weekend. Double dating with a friend who had a car was another option, but Dan longed to be the big shot with his own car. Besides, girls loved guys with cars.

Neither Mom nor Dad looked forward to the day the children would start dating. When kids went out without Mom and Dad, who would encourage them to make the right choices of activities and friends? But like all parents they had to hope the upbringing they gave their family and God's guidance would help us make good choices. It did, with a few bumps along the way.

Living in a small town, where everybody knew us, was a great help to Dad. If the boys got into any kind of trouble, the local police, who knew Dad, reported it to him and the boys were punished. The boys were more afraid of Dad than any law enforcement officer.

David's interest in cars gave Dad more than a few gray hairs. David always had old jalopies to fix up and constantly worked on them to keep them running. As a teenager, David's interest in animals took a back seat to his interest in cars. He wanted a garage where he could fix them up, and Dad was not about to give up his. So he let David clean out the lower level of the old barn and convert it into a garage to work on cars. David would often work late at night on his old jalopies. Then he'd get up early, go to school, his job after school and back out to work on his car. It was his regular routine. Considering himself the invincible teenager, he thought he didn't need to sleep much. He was too busy for rest.

One night Dad woke up around 2 AM and felt something wasn't right. He got up and looked out the kitchen window. Light was shining from a window in the barn. He couldn't believe David was still out there, working on his car. A little perturbed, he dressed and marched out to the barn. As he approached he heard a motor running. Well, he thought, at least he finally got it running. Dad would send David right to bed. When he opened the barn door, the carbon monoxide fumes about knocked him over. He yelled for David. No answer. Hurrying around the car he saw David, asleep on the front seat. He could barely awaken him. He switched off the car; got David to his feet and half carried him out the door. He spent a good part of the night walking David around the orchard in the fresh air until he became alert, and then took him in for some food. Working on the car at night alone was no longer an option for David. Dad sat at the table unable to eat, watching David eat breakfast thinking about how close he came to losing a son. He was sick thinking about what might have happened if he hadn't awakened. There was definitely a guardian angel watching over Dad's kids.

David's old cars kept him broke. The money he earned at his part-time job at the local feed mill barely covered insurance and parts to keep the cars running. Good tires were a luxury David could not afford. So, when a friend of David's from school, Jim, told him about some free tires he was delighted. Jim had an older brother who had totaled his car in an accident. Jim's brother was fine but his car was a complete loss. Talking with David during lunch period about the accident, Jim mentioned it was a shame the totaled car had a brand new set of tires on it. They happened to be the same size tires David needed for his car. Jim generously offered David the tires. They were on the wrecked car, which had been towed to the local Ford garage. All David had to do was jack up the car and take the tires.

His afternoon classes seemed to last forever. David couldn't wait for the final bell to ring, so he could get those tires. Imagine, free tires. What a break. Watching the clock, he was poised to run as soon as the bell rang. Out the door, books thrown into the back seat, he raced over to the Ford garage. There was the wrecked car, right where Jim said it would be. Four perfectly good tires, free for the taking. David got the jack from his trunk and started removing the tires. In broad daylight he was busy working.

One of the local cops pulled up behind his car. David just kept working. He knew the officer and didn't think anything of his being there. He was in a hurry to get the tires off the car so he could get to his after school job at Star Mill, next door.

As the policeman approached, he asked "What are you doing there, son?"

David answered, without looking up, "I'm taking these tires for my car."

He was shocked when the officer replied, "Then I guess you're under arrest."

After all, Jim said he could have the tires. To his surprise, the officer escorted him to his cruiser, took him to the police station, and did the unthinkable. He called Dad. He told Dad he had David at the station for stealing tires; he'd better come down. After the officer hung up the phone David waited, dreading the moment when Dad would arrive. Dad was so mad, thinking one of his kids would steal; he didn't take time to ask questions. He walked into the police station and read David the riot act in front of everyone. In small-town America in the 60's that was punishment enough for his gullibility. The officer let David go. When David got a chance to explain, Dad calmed down. Now he just wondered how David could be so easily misled.

In the 1960s' the country was involved in the Vietnam War. Mom was afraid her boys would be required to serve, and be sent to Vietnam. She waited for Dad during World War II, praying all the time he would come back to her. She and Dad did not want to send a son to war. But there was a draft, and when Dan turned 18 he was required to register. He was called to serve and although Mom was worried, she had to let him go, with prayers for his safety. Dan made all his arrangements. He quit his job, sold his car, and said goodbye to his family and friends. Mom and Dad took him to the bus station in Canton early in the morning. Crying, Mom waved goodbye as the bus pulled away. He arrived at the induction center in Cleveland with hundreds of other boys, all of them acting brave, like the men they were expected to be, but inside apprehensive about being soldiers. Standing in line for his physical, he thought about home and what might be happening there. He wished he were back there at his job instead of here with a crowd of strangers. When his turn came, the doctors discovered a lump on his lower abdomen. "It's a hernia," he stated matter of factually, as he stamped the paper and handed it to Dan. Dan glanced down to see, in big red letters across the paper; 'not eligible.' Dan looked at the doctor and said, "Hey, you used the wrong stamp."

"No, I didn't," said the doctor. "With a hernia you are not eligible." Thinking Dan was upset about not serving, the doctor explained, "If you sign up for the voluntary draft, that's a three year stint we'll fix the hernia and you will have six months off, then you'll report for duty and serve for two and a half years."

"Or?" said Dan.

"Or we'll give you a lunch voucher and a bus ticket home."

Dan opted for the ticket, threw the lunch voucher in the trash and hurried to the bus station, before anyone could change his mind. His new status was 1Y, which meant eligible for induction only in the case of national emergency or all-out war. Since Vietnam was never declared a war, he wasn't called up. At the bus station he called Mom, collect. When he told her he was coming home she cried and said, "Dan, don't do this to me; it's not funny." He had to convince her to pick him up at the bus station; he was really coming home.

Mom was happy she did not have to send Dan off to war, but soon David would be turning 18. Would he have to serve? When the birthdays were drawn for David's year, he was number 320. So he was spared the Vietnam experience. By the time the other boys reached 18, the Vietnam conflict was over and the draft was discontinued. None of Mom's sons had to serve. Dad didn't want the boys to experience the things he did during WWII. He had fought in the hopes his children never would.

Mom and Dad faced the same problems as other parents as the kids grew up. Like smoking. Some of the kids tried it. Dad smoked cigarettes when he was younger, but switched to cigars and a pipe when the coughing got too bad. How bad could smoking be if Dad did it? Mom never smoked. She told the girls it wasn't ladylike. That did not stop some of the girls from trying it. They weren't very smart about where they smoked. One day a group of them went in one of the big walk-in closets with a pack of cigarettes and matches. Marie, Gerard and Jerry were about to enjoy the delights of smoking. They needed a lookout and Jane was handy. They positioned her at the top of the stairs and told her to let them know if Mom started up the steps.

Sitting alone on the top step with nothing to occupy her time, Jane soon became bored. The only things she had to play with were her shoelaces. As she quietly played with them, tying and untying, Mom came up the stairs to see why it was so quiet. Mom was always suspicious of quiet; it wasn't natural in a home full of children. Jane didn't see her until she was right in front of her. Smelling the smoke, Mom put her finger to her lips to warn Jane not to say anything.

146

She went to the closet, opened the door and caught the guilty group in the act. She used the dreaded "Wait till your Father gets home" threat. Mom reported the find to Dad that evening. Sue, who usually participated in the group smoke, happened to be away that day and didn't get caught with the rest of them. When Dad lined them up for a whack, Sue just couldn't take the guilt; she confessed that she had participated in the past, when they had not been caught. Dad said, "Get in line." Sue got her whack with everyone else.

Mom and Dad did not have extra money for children to spend. We never got an allowance and seldom received cash. When we were old enough to need spending money, we were expected to earn it. We were taught to budget our money, spending it on things we needed, like clothes. And if we wanted fancy snacks or soda pop, we bought them, too.

We also gave half our earnings to Mom for "room and board." This was a real lesson in responsibility. We complained our friends did not have to give up half their earnings. Mom said she didn't care what other kids did. We had a responsibility to help with the family expenses, and we all had to pitch in.

Spending a Sunday afternoon, just Mom and me, was wonderful. I just wish she weren't in the hospital. Mom is ready to get back to Florida to see her kids down there. She is telling me how much she is dreading flying alone. I just can't let her do that, so I offer to buy a plane ticket and fly with her. Mom is delighted. She doesn't like to be alone. I don't blame her. This will give me a chance to visit with Jane, Tim, Vince, Andy and Ed while I am in Florida for a few days.

# Chapter Eighteen

## *Back to Florida*

When I call the airline for my ticket I am able to get a seat next to Mom. We have a smooth flight to Florida. There is only one stop, and we elect to stay on the plane since walking any distance is difficult for Mom. Dad and Jane are waiting at the airport when we arrive. It is a typical sunny, hot southern Florida day. When we arrive at the house, I settle in the guest room, and spend the rest of the morning visiting with Mom while Dad works in the yard. After lunch Mom takes a nap and Dad and I go shopping for groceries. All through the store he is looking for new things Mom can eat. Her diet is very restricted. No sugar because of her diabetes, no salt because of high blood pressure, and no fat because of her heart. There is not much left for her to eat. Dad shops very carefully for her, reading all the labels. We stop at the local feed store to buy a big bag of birdseed. Dad enjoys feeding the birds and Mom can watch the bird feeders from the living room window.

When we get home Dad takes me on the traditional vegetation tour, a trip around his yard. He really enjoys his yard and many citrus trees. He explains all the different fruit trees we don't have in Ohio. Besides the grapefruit and orange trees he has a star apple tree. I have never seen a star apple. It is an unusual fruit. It looks like a star when you slice it and tastes like an apple. I guess the farmer in him is still thriving. When we come back into the house Mom is up and sitting in a chair in the living room. She seems a little upset that Dad and I are enjoying some time together and she is left out. This is my first indication that her personality is changing. Mom is getting mean spirited. She is moody and seems to resent us sometimes. We later learned that the drug Halcyon that the doctor prescribed for her was changing her personality. When we discovered what was causing the problem, we talked to her doctor and he took her off the drug. After a short time she is more like herself. But her illness is taking its toll and she no longer seems to be the happy person we always knew.

In the evening Mom is not feeling well. The trip back from Ohio has been stressful for her. Dad takes her to bed and I hear her crying in their bedroom. As I approach the door to their room to see what is wrong Mom is saying, "Why is God making me suffer so? Why doesn't he take me and end my suffering?"

Dad calmly says, "You don't mean that. You're just tired. In the morning you'll feel better."

I back away from the door as he tucks her in and go to the guest room, closing the door. I sit on the edge of the bed and pray; "God. I don't know exactly what I am praying for. I want her to be better, but I know congestive heart failure is not reversible. I don't want her to suffer yet I can't imagine not having her here with us."

I know she is really sick and her heart is bad, but in front of her children she always tries to be brave. She never complains to us and always has a smile when she sees us. I realize, sitting here on the bed, that she is protecting us. She doesn't want us to worry about her. Here is a woman suffering terribly and she is still protecting her grown children from the heartache. After I have a good cry, I go back out into the living room. Dad is sitting in his favorite chair, reading the paper. He asks me if I am all right. I tell him yes. We don't talk about what happened in their bedroom and I have a feeling it was not the first time she had said that to him. We watch a little TV and then turn in for the night.

The next morning is Sunday and we attend Mass at Mom and Dad's church. After dressing for church I go into Mom's room. She is sitting on the bed wearing a light flowered dress. She looks small and frail, but she smiles as I walk into the room. No sign of last night's despair. I offer to fix her hair, and we talk as I curled it with a curling iron.

149

She thanks me for coming with her on the plane and we talk about everything but her illness. I offer to put a little foundation and lipstick on her face so she would have better color and when I finish she looks really nice. I give her the hand mirror so she can see the results. She's pleased and I'm happy to be able to give her a little pleasure.

At church, Dad parks by the door in a handicap space, since Mom can't walk very far. Jane and her family are at Mass, and Jane waves to Mom from across the church. After Mass we take Mom back to the car. Many people come over to greet her and remark how nice she looks. As I stand back and watch her accept the greetings from all her friends, and as they inquire about her health and her trip to Ohio, I reflect on how well liked she is and how sincerely people wish her well. I'm so happy they have their faith and these wonderful people around them.

We drive home and Dad fixes dinner. Here is a man who never cooked when I was a child, and now he can prepare an entire Sunday dinner. His role in the household has changed. He is now the one cleaning, cooking and shopping. After dinner Mom takes a nap and Dad and I try to make sense of all the medical bills and Medicare forms. What a mess of paperwork. It takes us all afternoon to figure it out together.

In the evening my younger brothers and their families come over to visit. They have not seen Mom since spring, when she left for Ohio. I watch as she is transformed. When the boys arrive she puts on a huge smile and never let on to any of them how sick she really is. I'm amazed at her ability to laugh and enjoy the kids and grandkids when she looks so tired. As each of them walks in, she lights up. She is right about her kids keeping her happy.

I spend part of the next day with Jane. We enjoy a walk on the beach and some time just having sister talk. I spend the evening with Mom as I think about going home the next day. I am sure if I leave I will never see her again. I try to memorize every word and gesture I can this last night in Florida. I watch her and listen to every word she says. I try to memorize her face, her voice and remember each mannerism. It takes all my resolve to laugh and enjoy the family when all I want to do is hug her to me and keep her safe. I think back on the times she and I didn't get along so well. When I was a teenager, I rebelled, as most teenagers do. But now I know how right she was about many of the things I couldn't understand then. With teenagers of my own I can relate to how she felt.

The next morning Mom rides along when Dad takes me to the airport. I hug Mom goodbye at the curb as she sits in the front seat of the car. I can't hold back the tears and neither can she. But she speaks to me as if I am a child and says, "No crying, I'll see you in May." It's amazing; I'm in my 40's and I feel like a little kid, faced with leaving a parent behind. I am sure I will never see her again. But I have to go. Home, husband, kids and a job wait for me in Ohio.

I call Mom as soon as I get home and the sound of her voice is reassuring. As the weeks and months go by it is easy to imagine her, like she used to be, full of life and constantly on the go. It is easy to believe she is better when I can't actually see her. When we talk on the phone she puts on that happy voice and makes me believe she's doing great.

After Christmas she announces her plane reservations are made and she will come back to Ohio in May. She is even willing to fly alone since there is no one who can fly with her. We're excited that we are going to see her again.

# Chapter Nineteen

## *Jobs*

Mom was right. She arrives back in Ohio in May, just as she predicted. She is frail and needs assistance, but she is here and very happy. We are all amazed. We try to spend as much time with her as possible. Half of her summer is spent in the hospital. At one point she suffers from a bleeding ulcer and we're sure we will lose her. But as always against great odds she pulls through. I really believe her desire to constantly be with her kids helps her hang on. Looking at her in the hospital bed, I cannot believe she will make it. But she does. She is a very strong-willed lady. We marvel at her resilience. But we grew up watching her do whatever had to be done without complaint. She and Dad taught us to persevere. They also taught us to work for what we wanted. Dad always says, "a little hard work never hurt anyone."

With so many kids in a family, everyone had to pitch in and help. Everyone had jobs to do. The girls were expected to help out around the house and the boys to work outside. On the farm, everyone helped with major jobs like harvesting hay, wheat and oats. Baling hay was a hard job but we enjoyed the smell of fresh-cut hay, as it lay in the field for three days to dry. The ride into the barn to store the hay was fun, except the times the wagon was overloaded and tipped over. There was always a bunch of kids riding on top a load of hay. When the whole thing went over, kids flew everywhere, arms and legs tumbling along with the bales of hay. Thankfully, no one was ever seriously hurt. God surely was watching over us.

At the end of each trip to the barn we threw the bales on a grain elevator for the ride to the highest part of the barn for storage. Most years we had plenty of hay to last through the winter.

Riding the old combine Dad bought at an auction was another story. Two kids sat on the wooden bench at the back right side of the combine. As the machine cut the grain, the stalks became straw and shot out the back of the machine onto the ground to be baled later. The grain came out a chute with two outlets located directly across from the bench. Our job was to attach a burlap grain bag to the first outlet pipe. As that bag was filling we attached another bag to the other outlet. When the first bag was full, we pulled a lever and the grain started pouring into the second bag. We unhooked the first bag, tied it shut with a piece of bailing twine, and shoved it down the chute at the very back of the combine. The grain bags weighed roughly 50 pounds. It took all the kid power we could muster to fight that bag over to the chute. We had just enough time to attach another bag before the second bag was full and we started the whole process again. There was a lever to pull to allow the bags to drop to the ground when we got to the end of the field. They were picked up later by the pickup truck. Two kids could handle the job, if they didn't get distracted watching wild animals, talking or just daydreaming.

If we didn't keep up with the job, grain would overflow and be wasted on the ground. The combine and tractor were so noisy, there was no way to warn Dad if we got behind. The pressure was on.

Hating the outdoors as I did, I also hated working the combine. It was hot and sticky. Chaff from the wheat and oats filled the air around us. It stuck to our sweaty bodies and flew in our mouth and throats. It was miserable work.

Sometimes we got a break. Relatives from the city came to the farm for the weekend. They loved working the fields. To them it was an exciting adventure, a real change from city life. Riding a hay wagon or combine, driving a tractor, helping with milking and feeding animals were fun, if you didn't have to do it all the time. I was happy to help cook or tend to the babies so they could enjoy themselves.

In the house we all helped with cleaning. Well, at least the girls did. Washing clothes and hanging them on the line outside, weather permitting, gave me a great feeling of accomplishment. After helping Mom, I often went down the lane to the neighbor's to help out. The Visnick family lived in the house across the road. They were poorer than us, and had a house full of little boys. Since her only girl was the baby, Ritha Visnick did not have help around the house. I did dishes, swept up, hung clothes on the line, or mopped the kitchen floor. In spite of having very little money, she paid me a few coins for helping. I thought I was rich. With the money I could go to the little corner store just up the road from our school and buy a candy bar or a box of salted pumpkin seeds. That was my first job. Helping Ritha. With a house full of little boys, no car or driver's license, Ritha wanted the company as much as the help.

Some days Ritha walked up our lane with her tribe of little guys to visit Mom. Ritha didn't have a television. So she and Mom sat together in our living room and watched their favorite daytime show, "Queen for a Day." It was a very popular game show in the 50's. Each day they featured three women contestants. They each told their sad stories of misfortune, trying to win a prize they desperately needed. One had a lot of kids and no washer and dryer. She talked about doing laundry by hand with a washboard. Another needed a stove or a new refrigerator. They told of being poor or ill, or caring for many children or less fortunate relatives. The stories were tragic. After the contestant told their story, the audience voted by applauding, as a meter was held in front of the camera, showing the television viewers the volume of applause.

Mom and Ritha voted for contestants they thought were most needy and sat there hoping their choice would win. When the winner was announced she was crowned "Queen for a Day." A crown was placed on her head and a red velvet cape draped over her shoulders and she was handed a beautiful bouquet of red roses. Then, as she cried tears of happiness, she was shown the prizes she had won.

Many times by the end of the half-hour show the contestants and audience were all crying. So were Mom and Ritha. They both dreamed of being on the "Queen for a Day" program and talked about what they would ask for if they got the chance.

When I was old enough to babysit other people's kids that became my source of income. Watching kids on weekends earned a few dollars each week for necessities. As soon as we were able to earn money Mom started charging "room and board." We gave her half of what we earned to help with groceries. With that many mouths to feed, even with raising some of our own food, the grocery bill was hard for Mom to handle. We didn't give up half of our earnings happily. We all considered it unfair, but pay we did. Mom said it taught us responsibility. We were also expected to give generously to the church on Sunday. Each of us had our own envelope for the Sunday collection. Mom would put change in our envelope. But when we earned money, we were expected to do our part to support the church.

With Nancy gone, I was the oldest and the first to get a real job. At 14, a freshman in high school, I got an after school job at a local Catholic nursing home, St. Joseph's Hospice. It was across the street from St. Louis School, in town. As kids, we were afraid of the place. It was a big brick building with overgrown bushes out front. In the back was a big walled garden area. We heard stories from other kids about the mean nuns who ran the place. We were afraid to go near the property since we were convinced the nuns lurked behind the walls of the garden just waiting for someone to stray onto the property so they could nab them. We didn't even dare ride our bikes down the alley beside the walled garden.

When my parents heard there was a job opening for the dining room after school they insisted I apply. With great trepidation I walked the mile from my house to the Hospice. I went through the back gate and into the building to see the nun in charge. I found my way in through the delivery entrance. I stopped the first person I saw, a maintenance man, and ask for the Sister in charge. I was instructed to wait on a chair in the hallway. After what seemed like forever, a tall nun in a flowing habit came hurrying down the hall. I was all of five feet tall and weighed about 90 pounds. I was pretty intimidated by this very large and formidable nun. After a short interview, I got the job. Not because I did well in the interview, but because Monsignor Dalmage from St. Louis told Sister I needed the work. She knew all about our large family, then numbering only 11 children. She made it quite clear she did not like me on sight. But she felt obligated to give me the job since Monsignor Dalmage was in favor of my working there. But I'd better work hard and be on time.

I went home and told Mom I had the job. She was so excited. Not only would I earn 35 cents an hour, I would also eat supper at the Hospice every weekday. Mom thought the best jobs in the world were jobs that not only paid you, but also fed you.

Every day after school, I rode the bus for an hour from Central Catholic High School in Perry Township to downtown Louisville. I went straight to the Hospice and worked in the dining room. The residents who were able to leave their rooms, came down for dinner on the lowest level of the building. I circulated around the tables and assisted anyone who needed help. After dinner, I cleared the tables, wiped them off, and set them for breakfast the next morning. Then I was permitted to eat dinner at a table in a small storage room. After eating, I helped the dishwasher. Dad came to pick me up when I was finished for the day. It really wasn't a bad job.

There was a priest staying at the hospice. I was introduced when I started the job but Sister warned me to stay away from him. She said he wasn't quite right upstairs and pointed to her head. I took this to mean he was a little crazy. I didn't know a priest lived at the Hospice. I was just as intimidated by priests as I was by nuns. Staying away from him would be easy.

Things were going well for the first couple of weeks. Then, one evening as I was clearing tables after dinner, the old priest came into the dining room. Being taught to always be polite, especially to the clergy I said, "Good afternoon, Father." He did not respond but approached me saying "Buttons." When he was within arms reach he started trying to unbutton my blouse. I was wearing my uniform from school. I pushed his hands away and escaped to the kitchen, thinking Sister was right, something was definitely wrong with his head. I continued working each day after school. A few evenings later while I was clearing tables, Father came into the dining room again. He kept saying only the word "buttons" and attempted to unbutton my blouse. This time Sister came into the room. She shouted, "Kathy!" Father jumped, turned and scurried from the room.

As Sister approached I could see she was angry.

"I told you to stay away from the priest!" She exclaimed.

"He came in here," I told her.

"That doesn't matter," she said. "You stay away from him. If I catch you with him again, you're fired. Do you understand?"

As she breezed out of the dining room I vowed to stay as far away from Father as possible. From then on I kept one eye on the door when I worked alone in the dining room. When he showed up I'd make a beeline for the kitchen where others were working and act busy until he left. He never followed me. One evening I was clearing the last table in the far corner of the dining room. My back was to the door and I was rushing to get finished. I had tons of homework that night and I was hurrying to get home as soon as I could. I wasn't watching for the priest. I heard a noise and as I turned around there he was, standing right behind me. I was cornered. He was between the kitchen and me. The kitchen door was about 35 feet away, and there was no route of escape. He started with the "buttons" again. As I struggled to keep him from unbuttoning my blouse while trying to get away, Sister appeared in the doorway. For a

157

split second, I was glad to see her. She started toward us with her habit flowing behind her. Father scampered away.

"What did I tell you about staying away from Father?" she demanded with hands on her hips.

I tried to explain but she shouted, "Answer my question."

"Stay away from Father or I'll be fired," I timidly replied.

"You're fired!" she said. "Get your things and leave." She hurried from the room leaving me standing there in shock.

I called Dad and asked him to pick me up early. When he asked why I was leaving early, I said I had been fired. By the time he picked me up he was so mad he was beet red. He had never been fired from a job in his life, and here was his first child, fired from her first job. I tried to explain but he wouldn't hear it. He was mad at me for a long time after that. But I was not pressured to get another job, which was a relief for me. After that experience, babysitting and school were enough for me.

Some of us tried to earn some spending money selling door to door. I tried selling greeting cards and stationery but I was too timid to make a good salesman. Dan got a job delivering detergent samples. The new detergent claimed to work in cold water and was called "Cold Power." Dan would ring the doorbell, drop the sample in front of the door, and yell "Cold Power" and run. Bravery was not our strong suit.

Some of the boys mowed lawns for cash. Jerry and Gerard got a job mowing at a local swimming pool, Starry High. They rode their bikes to the pool, mowed the grass around the area and rode the bikes home. Even such a simple job turned out to have some perils. There were some less than friendly dogs living between our house and the pool. They both rode their bikes with one hand, holding a big stick in the other to swat at the dogs.

When Dad started his cabinet shop many of the boys worked for him. They learned a trade and earned some money. Some of them stayed on at the shop after graduating from high school. The older ones became excellent cabinetmakers, like Dad. The younger ones worked in the shop, too. They were too young to work the big power saws or construct cabinets, but they could do clean-up work. Sometimes Dad brought the younger boys down to the shop after school to clean up. They could sweep up sawdust, stack wood and take scrap wood out of the shop. If Dad had to leave to bid jobs or get material, he put the younger ones in the care of the older boys. As soon as Dad was gone, the little boys got underfoot. No one could get any work done. This was irritating. It didn't take them long to lose patience with their younger brothers. They devised a solution to the problem. If, after a couple of warnings, the younger ones didn't settle down, Dan or David picked them up, sat them on a work bench and used a staple gun to staple their jeans to the bench. Andy, Ed and Tim were nailed down. They couldn't get off the bench or get underfoot. Sometimes they stapled their shirts and pants to the wall to keep them immobile. When Dad pulled back into the shop parking lot the younger boys would be set free. They couldn't tell Dad what Dan and David had done without incriminating themselves. It was the perfect solution.

Mom was always looking for a way to earn extra cash. It was impossible for her to work outside the home, but her experience during World War II gave her a taste of earning her own money. She and her best friend Barb Hoobler discussed ways to earn money. So many people gave us clothes; Mom had closets full of things that did not fit any of us. Barb and Mom thought, if people had so many clothes that were still usable maybe they would be interested in selling them. So they opened a store called the "Next To New" shop. They rented a storefront in our small town and advertised in the local paper. They offered to sell 'next to new' clothing on a consignment basis. People brought in clothing to sell. Barb and Mom marked the items and manned the store. After 90 days the owners of the cloths collected their money and took back any unsold items. Mom loved her little shop, but after a few years she tired of the work for very little pay and they closed it.

But Mom still got plenty of hand-me-downs from friends and family. When she protested, people said they didn't want the items and Mom could just throw away anything she couldn't use. This went against her nature. She did not throw away good clothes. Her solution was to rent an empty storefront in Canton for a single day. She chose a Saturday and, with the help of several little workers, she took boxes and bags of clothes to the storefront. She put an ad in the paper announcing a one-day rummage sale. Near the end of the day, rather than take unsold items home, she would put up a sign, "All you can fit in one grocery bag $1.00." Many people stuffed their bags full and Mom had very little to take home.

Mom was always coming up with a scheme to earn money. Dad listened and just shook his head. She wanted to open an ice cream stand, start a pet cemetery, and open a fruit and vegetable stand. The list went on and on.

Watching her laughing about all her schemes, as she says she still may open that ice cream stand, I wonder at her determination. She says she is bored since she cannot do much any more. I ask her what she would like to do.

"I want to learn to do embroidery. Like you do. I would love to use this time to make pretty things."

"I'll get you some easy things to start with." I tell her. "I'll bring them down next weekend and teach you how to do cross stitch."

It's the least I can do after all the things she taught me. But the things I learned from her are of much greater value than pretty stitching.

# Chapter 20

## *Saying Goodbye*

It is apparent this is the last summer Mom will spend in Ohio. She is very weak and spends a good part of the summer in the hospital. When she isn't in the hospital she sits on the screened in porch at Springwood. Whenever we visit she is rocking in her favorite chair. She always welcomes company. Mom loves to talk and tell stories about her life, her kids or her family. She enjoys having her kids around her. She once told me, "All I ask of God is that he let me live to see my children raised." They are all raised and she is happy.

However, she seems a little upset that it appears she will die before Dad. After all, most women of her generation outlive their husbands. I can see some resentment about that. I believe it's mostly the drugs. She is on some controversial anti-depressants and sleeping pills that are changing her personality.

She gives Dad fits. He has been taking care of her for the last few years, but nothing he does seems to please her. I've read that people who are sick often take their frustrations out on the closest person to them, their caregivers, and Dad is getting more than his share of grief from Mom.

As summer ends Mom comes to stay with me while Dad drives back to Florida. He wants to leave a few days before her flight so he can be there to pick her up when she gets off the plane in Naples. During her stay I really see how frail and helpless Mom had become. She was the rock that kept us on the straight and narrow, the person we went to for help. Now she needs help with everything. This is a woman who had the strength to raise 15 children, washed diapers for over 20 years, and got through many rough times while raising a rambunctious group of kids. She saw us through broken bones and broken hearts. She expected us to do what was right and become independent adults.

Now as I help her bath and get her meals, I see that our roles are reversed. She had taken care of me and all the other kids for so many years. Now she needs care.

I am so grateful for these last days of the summer we spend together. We have long talks and enjoy each other's company in my home. I am able to make her comfortable, as we share these pleasant days. Mom had never cared much for my husband. What man is good enough for any of her daughters? But during this stay she has an opportunity to talk with him one afternoon when I am napping. She let him know that he wasn't so bad after all, he was a good provider and helped produce and raise four of her grandchildren.

However, she tells him, he better get a railing on the back steps before she comes back next spring. She needs it to get up and down those stairs. He installed it a week after she left. I had to smile as I remembered the way her Mother used to tell my Dad what he should do around the house. How like Grandma she is.

Rose and I take her to the airport and put her on the plane for Florida. I pack a lunch for her to have on the plane. She doesn't care for the diabetic meals the airline provides. As we settle her into her seat on the plane, we tearfully kiss her goodbye and make her promise to call us as soon as she gets home. As Rose and I walk back to the car together, we both know we will not see Mom again.

The first weekend of December Mom gets worse. Dad takes her to the hospital on Tuesday. They admit her and make her as comfortable as possible. The next day the doctor comes in to see her and he doesn't look happy. As a matter of fact, he looks quite grim. He sits down beside Mom's bed and takes her frail hand in his.

"I have something to tell you," he says as he looks into her eyes.

"Mrs. Johanning, you have to understand something. You are dying. We have done all we can possibly do for you. Your heart is very weak. You are not going to live much longer."

He paused but Mom doesn't respond. She just looks at him with tears in her eyes.

He takes a breath and continues. "Mrs. Johanning, do you want to die here in the hospital or at home?"

"Home," she quietly responds.

"Then go home and don't come back here. We will not be able to do anything for you but make you comfortable. If you don't want to die here, with machines helping you breathe and tubes all over the place please stay at home."

"OK," is all Mom says.

The doctor makes sure she has prescriptions for painkillers that will help her be comfortable and sends her home on Thursday.

Mom calls each one of us when she gets home. She tries to sound as positive as possible and tell us how happy she is to be home and not in a hospital. She thanks us for the flowers and all our prayers. She tells us how much she loves us and misses us. We know what the doctor said, but Mom has beaten the odds for three years already. Surely our loving prayers would help her through this crisis.

When I say goodbye to Mom, I put down the receiver and have a good cry. Mom is not one to express her feelings. She is always reserved and lets her actions speak for her. We know we are loved by the way she cared for us and showed interest in the things we did. Always the no-nonsense person, she doesn't take time to express her feelings verbally. I feel the call I just received means she has surrendered to her illness. Her fight is almost over.

On Saturday, Jane and her husband Rocky bring the bikes they purchased for their kids' Christmas to Mom and Dad's. They are going to store them in their shed until Christmas, so the kids won't find them. Mom is up, sitting in a chair in the living room in good spirits. She jokingly tells Jane she is going to try out the bikes and go for a ride in the warm Florida sun. She always loved riding a bike. She almost seems like her old self. Jane leaves feeling good about her. She feels she will have Mom for one more Christmas.

# Chapter 21

## *Mom's with Nancy*

It is Sunday morning, December 13, 1992. I have tickets to the Canton Symphony Orchestra Christmas Concert and I am looking forward to the performance. The phone rings at about nine. I answer it, feeling a little trepidation. Mom is not doing well and this could be Dad. It was Jane, from Florida.

"Kath?" asks Jane.

"Yeah, Jane," I answer.

"I think this is it," Jane says, in a shaky voice.

"What do you mean?" I ask.

"I think Mom's dying this time."

"Jane, she has been this sick many times before. Why is this different?'

"It's just different. It just feels different. I really think we are going to lose her."

Jane is calling from Mom and Dad's home. Dad called her because he was scared and didn't know what to do. Mom was not responding to him.

Forever the optimist, I tell Jane, Mom has been near death several times in the last three years and always pulled through. I just don't want to accept it. We only talk for a few minutes when Jane has to go; Mom has called for her. I ask her to keep in touch.

I call Dan. I feel so helpless, so far away from Mom. We only talk for a minute. We don't want to tie up the line. I'm afraid to go to the concert for fear I would miss a call. I wouldn't enjoy it anyway. The phone rings again and it's Dan. Jane had called him. He is frantic. All we could do is wait.

About 10:30AM Jane calls again. Mom is gone. She has simply stopped breathing, quietly, peacefully. Jane said

165

she sat there, holding Mom's hand and telling her she was with her whenever Mom seemed restless. Jane looked up to heaven; tears in hers eye, and asked God to please take her and stop her suffering. Every time Jane touched her, she cried out as if in pain. Then the room grew quiet, Jane realized Mom was not breathing. Her first reaction was to tell God, "I didn't mean it. I want her back."

She ran to the door and shouted, "Dad, hurry I think this is it!" Dad ran in immediately and hurried to Mom's side. She didn't respond to him as he sat there, holding her hand and quietly talking to her.

After Jane tells me, I can't help but cry, but I know there are brothers and sisters to call. First I reach Dan. He burst out in tears and we can't even talk. We decide all the kids in Ohio should gather that evening at my house. We have to be together.

The calls are hard to make but being busy helps keep our minds occupied. There are other members of both Dad and Mom's family to notify and many friends of the family to call.

We can only imagine what is happening with the other kids in Florida. Plans are being made to leave for Ohio. Mom's body will be flown to Ohio for burial in St. Louis Cemetery. Dan and I purchased her "final piece of real estate," as she called it, a couple of years ago.

When everyone arrives at my house they have Mom's grandchildren and great grandchildren with them. It is a house full. Throughout the evening we hear about the plans everyone is making in Florida. Dad asks us to make arrangements with Paquelet's Funeral Home, here in Louisville. Dad has known the Paquelet family his entire life and he wants them to make the arrangements. We decided that Sue, Dan and I would go there first thing Monday morning.

Being together is such a comfort that no one wants to leave. But as it gets late we have to part with promises to keep everyone up to date on the plans.

The funeral will be held on Friday, with calling hours on Thursday afternoon and evening, giving everyone time to get here from Florida. Dad left as soon as the arraignments to fly Mom's body to Ohio were completed. The rest of the kids would follow.

Everyone will be staying at different houses. But we need a gathering place. That will be my house, since Dad will be staying with me.

On Thursday morning we meet at the funeral home for a private family viewing. Just the 14 kids and Dad. No husbands, no wives, or grandchildren. When it is time for the viewing, we all hold hands and walk in together. I really thought I had cried all I could over the last few weeks. But seeing Mom there in the casket starts fresh tears for everyone. Ed, the youngest, hugs me and says he feels bad for me because I had Mom the longest and the loss for me must be greater. I feel the opposite. He had Mom for the least years and I think his loss was greater. In reality, she is Mom to each of us. The loss and sorrow we feel is universal.

There are so many flowers that they have nowhere to put them. They are displaying them in every possible place. Floral arrangements were placed three deep down the entire length of the room. They have them in the hall, on the tables and in an adjoining room. What a wonderful tribute to Mom from the people who loved her. We had our family picture displayed near the casket. How proud and happy Mom looked in that picture. How she would have loved seeing all her kids together like this. We reluctantly left the funeral home to get ready for the long day ahead.

We gather at my house before the two o'clock calling hours and arrive at the funeral home together. The two hours goes fast as we visited with the people who cared about my mother and accept their words of sorrow and encouragement.

At four o'clock we gather back at my house for dinner. The food provided by well-wishers is a godsend. We are worn out and glad to have all the help.

At a quarter to seven I announce it is time to return to the funeral home. I feel like I am standing in for Mom as the leader of this group as I gather them up to leave.

We are not prepared for the crowd that greets us this evening. The Funeral home is filled and the line snakes through the various rooms and out the door. To know this many people loved and cared about Mom is a great comfort to us. As I look down the line of Mom's children, all greeting people, I can't help but feel proud of them. They are, as Mom wanted them to be, fine independent adults with families of their own.

The evening calling hours seem to end in no time. There is nothing like activity to help the time pass. Everyone goes home to try and get some sleep. Tomorrow we will say our final good-byes to Mom.

We held the Funeral Mass at St. Louis. I'm sure Mom can see her nine handsome sons, as they carry her casket to and from the church. I can imagine her looking proudly down from heaven at them, in their jackets and ties. The church is not quiet. As I said before, we do not cry quietly. After Mass, we follow the hearse to St Louis cemetery. There is a tent over the open grave with four chairs lined up. The boys carry the casket to the grave and gently set it on the supports. I sit down next to Dan and Dad with Jane on the other side of me, as all the other kids gather behind us. The priest waits until all the mourners are gathered to say the final prayers over her casket. When he is finished Dad stands up, places his hand on the casket and says. "So long, Ma."

That's more than Dan or I can take. We embrace and sob in each other's arms. These are the times when your faith helps you through. As I embrace Dan, the way I had when we were children, I thank God for him, and all of my brothers and sisters. Mom will live on in each one of us and each of our children. We are here because of her deep faith and her belief that "God never gives you more than you can handle." With God's help, we can handle this.

After several minutes we pull ourselves together. People are walking back to their cars. As I stand to leave I can't help but think about the question Uncle Vince, one of Mom's younger brothers, asked me as he hugged me at the funeral home last evening. "Who do you think called Alice to heaven, Kathy? Nancy or Grandma Foltz?" I believe they welcomed her into heaven together. I will miss her so, but I take comfort in knowing she is with her Mother and her little Nancy again.

Alice's children